BLESSED BY THE BOYS

BLESSED BY THE BOYS

◆

THE TRUTHS OF GOD MANIFESTED IN FAMILY EXPERIENCE

Ron Branch

iUniverse, Inc.
New York Lincoln Shanghai

BLESSED BY THE BOYS
THE TRUTHS OF GOD MANIFESTED IN FAMILY EXPERIENCE

iUniverse books may be ordered through booksellers or by contacting:

iUniverse
2021 Pine Lake Road, Suite 100
Lincoln, NE 68512
www.iuniverse.com
1-800-Authors (1-800-288-4677)

ISBN-13: 978-0-595-39356-5 (pbk)
ISBN-13: 978-0-595-83752-6 (ebk)
ISBN-10: 0-595-39356-X (pbk)
ISBN-10: 0-595-83752-2 (ebk)

Printed in the United States of America

Contents

INTRODUCTION

"Blessed By The Boys" prioritizes the precious truths of God manifested through the six sons of the Branch family. Things that they said, things that they did, and even things they put our whole family through have been effectively used by God to reveal more of Himself. Therein lies the true blessing.

This anecdotal collection categorically affirms the following spiritual truths concerning God:

1. God is worthy of adoration and praise;

2. God' principles are practical;

3. God gives great comfort;

4. God emphasizes the priority of the church;

5. God's salvation is too great to be neglected;

6. God confronts our inadequate spiritual perspectives;

7. God's truths are not paralyzing;

8. God gives great blessing;

9. God is always the answer to all our questions;

10. God helps us grieve well;

11. God wants us to be victorious.

The stories that may open eyes and hearts to these truths certainly give the outsider opportunity to deduce particular and peculiar characteristics of the Branch family. However, emphasizing God so that the spiritual good of the reader may trust God more is the ultimate goal. The gamut of humor, seriousness, and tragedy within the Branch family experience makes possible spiritual edification for all in the name of and for the glory of God.

Ron Branch
April 7, 2005

1

GOD IS WORTHY OF ADORATION AND PRAISE

○ ○

"THOU ART WORTHY, O LORD, TO RECEIVE GLORY, AND HONOR, AND POWER"

—(REVELATION 5:11)

THE WRECK
(2-24-00)

Many times and in many ways, we are reminded over and over by God how great He is. Sometimes He reminds us how great He is in subtle ways. Sometimes it becomes apparent how great He is in adverse circumstances. Sometimes remembrance is stimulated in subtle ways during adverse circumstances.

One Saturday afternoon, our son, Eran, drove our car to Huntington with a friend. During the trip, Eran wanted his companion to listen to a Gospel song on a cassette tape, which was recorded by the local, well-known group named "Eternity." After the song played, Eran disengaged the tape, leaving it partially exposed inside the deck door, to listen to the radio.

Later that evening, the two were back with us at the house for a while. About 7:30 PM, sleet began to fall, and it was not long after that Eran set out to take his friend home.

However, on a stretch of road along a certain rock cliff, Eran lost control of the car on the slick road. The car slipped into the ditch, hit a rock, and flipped onto the top, which was considerably smashed.

Miraculously, both incurred only scratches on their hands. When I arrived at the scene and saw the extensive damage to the car, I was very thankful to God that neither my son nor his friend was seriously injured or killed. Many people who passed the accident in the lines of backed up traffic also commented how horrified they were to see such a severe accident, yet were very grateful to learn that the two were in no physical danger. God wonderfully spared our children, and we are very much aware of the grace He directed our way during this adverse incident.

But, the story becomes more compelling.

With the arrival of the police, Eran went to retrieve the insurance and registration papers from the glove compartment of the crushed car. As he got down on his knees to reach inside, he heard music playing and someone singing.

At that very moment, the quartet's rendition of "HOW GREAT THOU ART" was playing. Apparently, during the accident, the tape got kicked back into the player. The timing of the song as Eran crawled into the wreckage was an impeccable reminder of a standard yet spectacular spiritual truth.

Through it all, in a subtle way during adverse circumstances, God on this particular night communicated to us in a grand way how great He is. On that road which had become slick so quick, God was great enough to be with our children.

As that car slipped and slid into the ditch, God was great enough to be with our children. When that car was stopped by the rock and flopped on its top, God was great enough to be with our children.

It was not a matter of coincidence. It was not just chance or happenstance. It was not a matter of luck. It is purely a matter of fact and record that God was great in **"THE WRECK."**

With a sense of awe, I aver how great God is in His deliverance. The Scripture affirms it, too, in that "The angel of the Lord encampeth round about them that fear Him, and delivereth them" (Psalms 34:7).

You see, there ever remains one constant in life—sometimes, bad things happen to God's people. We live in a world in which accidents happen, in which evil is prevalent, in which disease afflicts, in which death comes to all. We live in a world in which oppression and depression often press the lives of God's people. Insecurity and sadness stick and burst our bubbles of blessing and joy.

Even the Apostle Paul, that great saint of God's, revealed that there had been a time in which he got pressed out of measure, above strength, even despairing of life. But, he said that God was great in His deliverance. God's deliverance was so great and so astounding that it was as though God had raised him from the dead!

We, too, can sing how great God is with deliverance in the midst of all the wrecks that happen to us in life. God's proven greatness undoubtedly breeds greater trust in Him. "O taste and see that the Lord is good: blessed is the man that trusteth in Him" (Psalms 34:8). God gives deliverance to His people in every circumstance of life. It is a spiritual truth onto which every saint may hold.

However, the accident scene led me to consider one further matter about the greatness of God's deliverance.

I see in "The Wreck" something of a personal nature. I know that for myself there is a wreck that I am going to have at some point in the future as the Lord delays His coming. That wreck will be physical death.

But, I am confident in the greatness of God that, when the time comes, He will be great in delivering me through His powerful salvation. Eternal life in the glories of Heaven is my eternal destination. Because of the greatness of God, Death cannot hold me back, Satan cannot take me down, hell will not be my home.

All of the universe will hear the sounds of my voice, "Then sings my soul, my Savior God to thee; HOW GREAT THOU ART, HOW GREAT THOU ART!"

WHEN THE CHILD COMPLIMENTS THE FATHER

"Here, Dad, I wrote this for you."

Our third son, Eran, a high school junior at the time, walked over and handed me a paper on which he had typed something. I had just gotten home from church, and was chatting with his mother.

As I read through the poem he had written about me, it made me very proud. He complimented his father. Sometimes, parents need for their children to reflect and communicate their perspectives of Mom and Dad. In this case, it re-assured me that perhaps my life has a beneficial effect on the boys we are raising to be men for the next generation. I remember how invaluable the model of my father has been to me over the years of my life.

Eran wrote:

THE SERVANT

A stout little man with traces of gray,
Takes his place in the pulpit and bows his head to pray.
At the start of his message, so humbly he speaks,
But, you see the tension mounting and the red in his cheeks.
As he takes off his coat, this man begins walk'n,
You better believe now that God's doin' the talk'n.
Now his finger shoots skyward, and he lets out a shout,
The sleepy awake, and the skeptics can't doubt
That this man is for Jesus; he's a "tool" of the Lord.
Then he calls the pianist and she strikes a Heavenly chord.
There's a gleam in his eye when a sinner is saved,
As their life is turned around and in Christ's blood they are bathed.
And, at the close of the service, he gives a handshake and smile,
And you know God is walking by his side every mile.

I will treasure this poem for the rest of my life. But, while this treasure is specifically mine, it is spiritually suggestive to all.

What Eran did was that he complimented his father. What Eran put into his own words reflects the stability of an intimate relationship he shared with me. His words mirrored his love and appreciation for who his father is and what his father does. Eran unwittingly knotted another tie in the Branch family cord, and, at the same time, threaded through our strong family unit another string into the fabric that holds society together.

But, through the scope of a broader spiritual perspective, note also how effective and beneficent it is when you, as a child, compliment your Father. In other words, our Heavenly Father deserves our compliments. It is critically important that the Christian child look to reasons and for ways to compliment our Heavenly Father.

The Psalmist poetically complimented the Father. "Bless the Lord, O my soul: and all that is within me, bless His holy name./Bless the Lord, O my soul, and forget not all His benefits" (Psalms 103:1-2). He cites many complimentary facts about the Father, who the Father is, and what the Father does (103:3-19). Then, he calls on the angels to compliment the Father (v20), the hosts of people to compliment the Father (v21), and the ministers to compliment the Father (v21). He concluded just as he started with the exhortation, "Bless the Lord, O my soul."

Do you as a Christian child compliment our Heavenly Father?

We should compliment our Heavenly Father whenever we have opportunity. We should speak complimentary of Him when we are around others.

My mother bought and gave to me for Christmas 1998 a bright yellow tie made by a company whose motto is "For the Body of Believers." The tie is so bright that I look like a huge, portable lamp stand with the light on when I wear it. When I first received the tie, I commented that I would not often wear it, and then only out of loving respect for my mother.

But, on this tie are the words "Modeling Jesus." I have found that when people notice the tie and comment about it, opportunity is present to point out the name of Jesus, and to speak complimentary about the blessedness of Jesus. The effect is uncanny.

Furthermore, we should often compliment our Heavenly Father for His free gift of salvation. God has given to man the opportunity for salvation. God does for us what we cannot do for ourselves. Blessed be the name of Almighty God for remembering us when we do not deserve His consideration. "What is man, that thou art mindful of Him? And the son of man, that thou visitest Him" (Psalms 8:4).

Complimenting our Heavenly Father is an integral part of worship. It is important for us to prayerfully acknowledge the good of God's providence directed toward us. It is important for us to assent in worship that He is holy, righteous, and just. While it is true that God does not have an innate need to hear compliments from us, it is equally true, by contrast, that we need to compliment Him.

The point is that as God's children we should willingly compliment our Heavenly Father. It is indicative of a loving, intimate, and stable relationship that threads the love of God not only through our personal lives, but also through the lives of others very much in need of Him.

I thanked Eran so much for the poem. I have it framed on display in my study.

I still love him and miss him so.

I THANK GOD FOR THE MAN

Someone once said it ought to be a law that people should not experience car problems or accidents when they go on vacation.

However, regardless of how we maintain our vehicles, or how carefully we strive to drive, car problems do afflict many who look forward with excited anticipation about having a brief respite from work and daily routine. Car problems when on vacation are especially disconcerting, adding unwanted stress and anxiety.

Thus it was for the Branches 2000 vacation excursion.

Terry, the younger boys, and I set out on a Tuesday for a variety of vacation destinations. The plan for our two older boys was to finish their workweek employment, and meet us in Mt. Airy, Maryland at Mom Barnard's on Friday evening for our annual trek to Ocean City, Maryland.

But, misfortune literally blew out our rendezvous plans for that day.

As the boys drove U.S 50 near Pennsboro, WV, over an hour from home, the right rear tire blew out. I had just bought a new set of tires for this vehicle in May in preparation for our July vacation.

Unfortunately, as they set about to make the change, they found to their chagrin that the spare was flat. Yes, my fault for not ensuring that detail!

But, the providence of God watched out for our sons in their stranded circumstances. God sent a man in a pickup truck. He was a good man. He was a man who had a heart to offer help. This man took care of my boys.

I was 300 miles away unaware that they were experiencing a problem. Even if I could have known immediately about the blow out and the flat spare, 300 hundred miles separation would have yet posed a problem in terms of discomfort and vulnerability after sunset. With all the violence that goes on, you can understand why I am grateful to God for the man He sent to help.

The man was on his way home from work. Apparently, he had put in many hours of labor that day. Yet, he took the time to take the spare tire to a place for repair. When he returned with the tire sometime later, he did not ask for money. He did not fuss about the time he had invested with them. Rather, he helped them put on the tire, and ensured that they were back on the road safely.

The boys thought it best to return to home. From there, they called and told me what had happened. Unfortunately, they did not ask for any particulars from the man concerning his name or where he specifically lives. I would have thanked him personally for his good Samaritan-like deed if they had gotten that information.

I do not know the man's name, but I thank God for the man.

Have you ever had problems along the road?

By contrast, life is often compared as a road we travel. We like to compare the twist and turns of traveling a road to the situations with which we are confronted in life. We contrast the potholes and bumps in a road to the adversities of life. Our road has steep mountains to ascend, and ditches into which we often slip. Sometimes, we refer to running out of gas. As we are apt to describe it, our road in life is full of travel circumstances that often leave us stranded, broken-down, and in need for help.

That is why God has sent to us a Man to give us gracious roadside assistance. It is said that this Man is the Master of the sea. But, undoubtedly, this Man is also the Master of the road. The Man's name is Jesus Christ.

He helps us because He is good. He does not fuss because of what He does for us. He has labored long and hard that we might experience His good for here and now, as well as for eternity.

Along your road, are you presently broken down with hurt and disappointment? The Man is there to make the necessary repair, and to get you back on your way.

Along your road, have you slipped into the ditch of discouragement? The Man is there to pull you out, and to get you back on your way.

The Man always arrives in a timely manner to assist us when we are stranded along our road of life. But, it is uncanny what He can to and for our road from that point forward.

Says the Scripture, "An highway shall be there, and a way, and it shall be called The way of holiness. No lion shall be there, nor any ravenous beast shall go up thereon. It shall not be found there. But the redeemed shall walk there. And the ransomed of the Lord shall return, and come to Zion with songs and everlasting joy upon their heads. They shall obtain joy and gladness, and sorrow and sighing shall flee away" (Isaiah 35:8-10).

There is something about the Man that vastly improves our road conditions for the days to come when we permit Him. Our roads become more scenic with the glory of God. Our roads become safer with the protection of God. Our roads become more joyful with the blessings of God.

He is able to do this for us because the Man says He is the way (John 14:6). He is the way because He paid the way. He is the way because He paved the way. He is the way because He proved the way.

I thank God for the man He sent to help my boys stranded along U.S 50. But, I also thank God for the Man, Jesus Christ, who was sent to help us all as we travel the road of life toward eventual eternity.

SOMETIMES IT IS NOT GOD'S WILL FOR US TO SING

Our sons and I have been singing gospel music together for many years now. Since we are all not under the same roof any longer, we do not get to sing as often as we did. But, times we are together, we make it a point to sing at church. We figure it is God's will for us to do so.

Such was our plan for one Sunday in particular when all the boys were home. But, something happened during our practice time on Saturday evening.

While we worked on a new song, Keithen made a critical comment about Eran. To make matters worse, Ron added to the slam. Eran took umbrage, and, as he left the church, he said he would never sing with Keithen and Ron again. I then fired a couple of salvos at Keithen and Ron for bickering us out of a practice session.

Though at home I tried to persuade Eran otherwise, he still refused to yield. But, it was after our conversation I began to sense that, indeed, for some reason or another, it was not God's will for us to sing that Sunday morning. I did not press the issue any further.

Doing the will of God should be the Christian's utmost concern, for we know that the plans and purposes of God are of primary consequence.

Nonetheless, the will of God is a difficult matter to discern accurately at times, particularly when it involves our concern to administer the tenets of God's kingdom. Our personal agenda may in fact do harm rather than accomplish the good we perceive our ministry will bring.

Consider the experience of the Apostle Paul and his ministry of preaching the Gospel.

Paul apparently had a missionary agenda. He, along with his co-laborers, positioned themselves "to preach the Word in Asia" (Acts 16:6). But, the Holy Spirit manifested the realization that it was not God's will.

Was it not God's will for him to preach, Paul could have asked? Could not the people of Asia have benefited from hearing the Gospel? Paul could have insisted on his own agenda, but he yielded to the expressed will of God.

Next, Paul headed into the direction of Asia Minor. But, once again, circumstances, according to the Holy Spirit, indicated that Paul's will concerning evangelism was not God's will.

Finally, Paul discerned the direct will of God (Acts 16:9-10), the significance of which enforced the Gospel of Christ in a movement westward among the nations of the world.

In retrospect, can we not see that the message of Christ is strong even in our own country in part because of Paul's unwillingness to push his own perceived agenda to do what he found out was the will of God?

Consider, furthermore, the heated discussions between Paul and Barnabas about the use of Mark. Acts 15:39 reveals, "And the contention was so sharp between them, that they departed asunder one from the other." Yet, God's will prevailed through it all, and, eventually, Paul realized had Mark had matured and was successful as a minister of the Gospel.

The point is clear. We have to be mindful to perceive the will of God even in adverse circumstances. Sometimes that is the only way God can get us out of the way so He can achieve His way.

Anyway, the next morning at church, the Lord rather assured me from what I saw that it was not His will for us to sing. God moved powerfully in certain lives that consumed the whole of the worship service.

However, five minutes before the start of the evening service, Ron and Keithen walked over to Eran, who sat in a pew waiting for the service, and said to him, "Let's sing." Eran got up without objection, we stepped to the fellowship hall for a quick warm-up, and we sang harmoniously before the church.

God is so good! Even more so, He is so right!

WOULD YOU BE WILLING TO LOOK UNDER THE COKE MACHINES?

When it comes to money, we never know what our boy, Micaiah, is going to come up with next, particularly when it comes to his technique of finding loose change. The family had been telling me about his success, but it took me by surprise the first time I witnessed first hand his aggressive, unabashed efforts.

We took a family trip to Ada, Ohio, to visit Keithen, who was in his junior year of pharmacy studies at Ohio Northern University. Micaiah was nine years-old. Along the way, we stopped at a rest stop on Route 33 just north of Columbus.

The boys had been dozing in the back seat of the car. But, when I shut down the car engine, Micaiah popped up, surveyed the situation with his sleepy eyes, and then energetically exclaimed, "Oh, boy! Pop machines!"

With that, he swung open the car door, and sprinted shoeless in banshee mode toward the row of pop machines situated near the facility doors.

I honestly had no idea what he had in mind, but I was distressed about his undisciplined dash from the car.

In an instant, he fell to his knees and started peering underneath the machines. I was starting to feel embarrassed because of the way other visitors were looking at him.

"Micaiah!" I called sharply while marching briskly toward him. "What are you doing? Get off the concrete!"

He did not hear a word I said. "Wow! Look what I'm finding!" By the time I got to him, he had snared five quarters and a dime from under the pop machines. "Hey, Dad, look! I'm $1.35 richer!" Despite my chagrin, I was somewhat impressed with the result.

Do you ever drop to your knees and reach under pop machines for loose change like that? Would you consider doing it? Micaiah is absolutely the first person I have ever seen making such a search.

Most likely, people regard genuflecting before a pop machine for a change search as something beneath them. As a matter of fact, I have seen people refuse to pick up a penny from the ground simply because it was "just a penny." If that had been the case with Micaiah, he would not have found that well-conditioned 1905 Indian head penny on the beach one summer.

But, the whole of the consideration brings our attention to an attitudinal problem many people seem to have about the holy things of God. It is as though the search for the spiritual riches of God is beneath them.

When is the last time you have knelt before God in search of understanding from Him about a verse of Scripture? How often do you seek Him out concerning His will for your life? Are you faithful to turn aside from the pursuits of life to respectfully honor His command to worship? Do you seek Him out everyday for all your needs, wants, and concerns? Unfortunately, it appears from the mindset people exhibit that too often the search for the treasures of God is not only embarrassing, but, an option not worth the effort.

The Scripture states that if we are willing to seek the things of God, like one who searches for silver and digs for deep treasure, we will be profoundly blessed. "Should not the people seek unto God?" Isaiah asked. Jesus said, "Seek ye first the Kingdom of God and His righteousness, and all these things shall be added unto you." The writer of Hebrews avers that God is a rewarder of those who diligently seek Him.

Why should we be hesitant and abashed to approach the God of Heaven to plum the depths of what He has in store for us? It only makes us richer when we do.

On our way home, we stopped to re-fuel at a gas station near Circleville, Ohio, on Route 23. Just as soon as the car stopped, Micaiah popped up, and exclaimed, "Oh, boy! Look at all those pop machines!"

Cha-ching!

2

GOD'S PRINCIPLES ARE PRACTICAL

○ ○

"THOSE THINGS WHICH YE HAVE BOTH LEARNED, AND RECEIVED, AND HEARD, DO: AND THE GOD OF PEACE SHALL BE WITH YOU"

—(PHILIPPIANS 4:9)

PLAYING WITH RATS IS A DANGEROUS PASTIME!

It is with permission in hand from my darling wife, Terry, that I relate this account to you, but I do so in fear and trembling because of the general mindset of many women concerning rats and mice. You just cannot tease women who are afraid of them.

My mother, who was visiting through Christmas holidays with us at the time, and our son, Eran, were in the kitchen one Sunday morning when they happened to see a small rat skirt the baseboards and disappear under the dishwasher.

My beloved wife, Terry, though normally strong in character and spirit, is utterly mortified by rats and mice. Consequently, she tensed up considerably when told about the sighting. Although only minutes from leaving for Sunday morning church, she immediately dispatched Eran to Wal-Mart in search of D-Con for rats.

Instead, Eran came home with pellets for mice.

When he returned, Terry was chagrined because she wanted the most potent potion possible for rats. Pellets for mice did not hack it as far as she was concerned. She had made sure she had given him enough money for rat poison. His purchase was incorrect and insufficient as far as she was concerned.

That was Eran's first mistake.

However, little did Terry suspect that her third-born son had pocketed the change saved from the price difference, and had also bought a battery-operated toy mouse he had seen on sale at a post-Christmas price.

After church, twelve were present at our house for lunch, including Ron and our daughter-in-law, Holly, my Mom, Mandy Blake, Kate Lowe, and the rest of the Branch brood.

After the blessing, Holly and I went to the living room and chatted, waiting patiently while lunch plates were prepared in the kitchen by our hungry group.

Suddenly, fear-laced shrieking and raucous laughter simultaneously rattled the rafters. I jumped to my feet with a start, and, as I entered the foyer, Terry dashed by and positioned herself on the upstairs steps trembling, eyes ablaze with fright, yet her countenance fist-flexed with anger.

It was then I looked into the kitchen to see a little toy mouse running its to-and-fro course across the kitchen floor.

Eran had pulled the toy from his pocket, turned it on, and set it at Terry's feet. That was the boy's second mistake.

All six of the Branch boys were having a big time at their mother's expense. Micaiah and Jamin were particularly delighted as they playfully chased after the mechanical creature.

With difficulty, I coaxed Terry back into the kitchen to eat. But, she was mad at her sons, especially and extremely so at Eran. The mirth of our family gathering was seriously marred because of the mousy mayhem which had been inflicted on her.

The afternoon hours passed with little more said about Eran's little prank, although Terry remained visibly shaken from the exposure of it all.

But, this is not the end of the story.

That evening at church, the Lord seemed to shower our worship service with blessing. But, unfortunately, it sometimes does not take too much humanity to suddenly resurface and spoil a good spiritual experience with the Lord.

After church, several groups stood in the sanctuary talking and basking in the spiritual afterglow. One of the groups included Terry, Eran, and about ten other ladies. I stood at the door talking with a couple of the deacons.

Unexpectedly, a shriek suddenly pierced the sanctuary. It was Terry. I saw her back pedal across the center aisle, hands clasping her jaws in apparent fright. In the next instant, her composure turned to anger, and she briskly walked out.

Eran had pulled that toy mouse out of his pocket and had exposed it to his mother in front of the other ladies while the rat story was being recounted. "Hey, Mom, look here!" he had said.

That was his third and final mistake of the day.

Once again, Eran had frightened, angered, and embarrassed his mother. The other women turned on the boy. The icy glares and stern reprimands he received from those ladies were well deserved. He also heard from me in due course.

I can imagine that most of the ladies who read this account feel with and for Terry, while frowning on Eran's pernicious prank on his mother as unconscionable.

But, more importantly, Eran's prank deservedly landed him in the doghouse with Terry. When a son has his mother seriously mad at him, it is not a good situation if one expects to eat and get their clothes washed.

Nonetheless, while the question was oft repeated during the week how Eran could have had the audacity to tease Terry so, there is a certain spiritual matter about which to concern ourselves in light of it.

A distinct contrast in this episode is found by way of general observation about people, because it is clear that we often have a playful mentality concerning spiritual matters.

We admit it, do we not, with trite references. When it comes to sporting about with spiritual issues, do we not often characterize ourselves as "playing with fire?" Do we not often "dance with the devil?" Do we not "play church?" Do we not "toy around with God?"

Has it ever occurred to you that God is very willing to reciprocate our inconsiderate and disrespectful playfulness concerning attitude toward Him?

Consider the discovery of this truth in I Samuel 5.

The Philistines must have been giddy with excitement when they captured the Ark of the Covenant from the Israelites. With great sport, the Philistines took the Ark to one of their five major cities, Ashdod. It was there that the Ark was set in the temple of Dagon, the fish god. Oh, what fun they must have planned at the expense of the God of Israel. Heathen laughter at Israel's God must have reverberated throughout the town.

But, God laughed back at them. God reciprocated in several ways. God first slapped the image of the Philistine god, Dagon, off his perch, much to the surprise of those disillusioned religionists who rejected the truth of God. Second, God slew many of the people who were so willing to jeer at Him. Third, He afflicted the living with disease. And, fourth, with the imagery of what Eran did to his mother before us, God pulled mice out of His creative coat pocket, and set them at the feet of the Philistines.

There were mice everywhere. The Bible says there were enough mice so as to "mar the land" (I Samuel 6:5). Undoubtedly, there was a great reaction generated in the people because of those tiny, furry, creatures creeping and slinking along the baseboards of their lives.

Suddenly, the Philistines did not want to play around with God anymore.

All too often do people regard the things of God, in so many terms, as ratty and mousy. Many tinker with the integrity of God. Many pooh-pooh the priority of Scriptural principles. Many scoff at the love of Christ. Many turn deaf ears away from reminders about the judgment of God. Many joke at the prospect of splitting hell wide open.

In His time, and in His way, however, God will cause the mouse to turn and run in their direction. He makes it clear, "I will laugh at your calamity; I will mock when your fear cometh."

Be mindful that, if you get ratty with God, you will reap the consequence.

One more thing—Eran wound up having company in the doghouse.

Not long after, Terry and I spent an evening re-arranging our room for a piece of new furniture. In a corner, I saw a small, brown football, which I picked up.

I couldn't resist the temptation. I lobbed it in her direction as I yelled loudly, "Oh, no, Terry! Another big rat!"

Woof! Woof! The big dog ain't so smart, either!

THE GUY OUTSIDE YOUR WINDOW MAY SHOOT IF YOU MOVE!

I had a difficult time getting to sleep one night. I got home about 11 PM, and, after a milk and banana snack, I hit the sack.

But, my mind just would not slow down for sleep. Eventually, I went down to the TV room to recline in the Lazy-Boy.

About 1 AM, Eran came in and cranked out the other Lazy-Boy beside of mine. We sat together in the dark for a minute before he asked, "What's the matter, Dad? Can't sleep tonight?"

"Nope, not tonight, son. I just can't get settled down," I replied.

"You ought to try what I do sometimes when I can't sleep," he offered. "I just think that there is some guy standing outside my window waiting to shoot me if I move a single muscle. That way, when I focus long enough on being still, I go right off to sleep."

I got a chuckle that Eran had such a mental solution for sleep. At the time, he planned to study psychology at college, and I told him to consider it for a case study analysis when he learned to diagnose the ramifications of such inner-self revelations.

Undoubtedly, people think in weird ways to help them deal with their varied circumstances.

But, all of this is powerfully suggestive of an important spiritual truth for the Christian, because what and how we think do make a vital difference to our well-being.

It is common for all that our minds sometimes whir over problematic situations. In the process of dealing with them, however, circumstances are compounded when our minds begin to create reasons for worry and concern. We allow ourselves to image a variety of unlikely scenarios that build stress and anxiety.

The longer we dwell negatively on our concerns the more adversely it affects us. For example, one of the reasons people have back problems is sometimes related to persistent emotional tension.

But, the Scripture says, "Be anxious for NOTHING!" It does not suggest that we may be anxious for some matters. Rather, it stipulates that we need not and should not be anxious for anything.

Imagine, if your will, sitting in a dark room of personal despair, and the Apostle Paul takes the chair beside of you, inquiring what your problem is.

You begin to bare your soul. "Oh, I am just worried to death! My problem is making me physically sick. I cannot eat. I cannot sleep. I just do not know what I am going to do. What did I ever do to deserve this?"

Paul then responds, "Let me suggest you do what God says, 'Whatever things are pure, lovely, or of good report, if there be any virtue or praise, THINK ON THESE THINGS.' Now, my friend, this is what I do, because it helps me focus on trust in God. I have found that it makes things go a lot better when I spiritually rely on Him and His power in my life."

There is absolutely no reason why a Christian should be bummed out with worry to the point your days and nights are botched! This is true, because God gives His peace, which sterling spiritual quality is described as passing all understanding.

The peace of God is a powerful stabilizer because it "keeps your heart." The peace of God is a powerful sedative because it "keeps your mind." Dwell on it today.

At Wednesday evening Bible study the following day, I related Eran's suggestion to the congregation at hand. Eran later told me an adult approached him after church and said, "It also works if you think that fella is under your bed!"

People sure think in weird ways.

DO YOU REALLY WANT TO DEAL WITH THE MESS?

Terry left the boys and me one Friday—

Of course, it was for the purpose of being able to baby sit the best grandson in this whole, wide world, Justus E. Branch, for a week on behalf of Ron and Holly, who live near Martinsburg, WV.

In the meantime, however, things changed dramatically for the three Branch brothers who are still a part of our present household.

You see, Terry is a loving mother who works hard to maintain a clean house for her sons. While she is careful to teach them in-home responsibility, she more often than not restores the messes left behind by the boys. She is prone to retrieve bowls and glasses from TV room snacks. She returns sandwich items to the refrigerator. She always does the dishes. Personally, I would utilize the manpower more often if I were she.

But, for this particular week, the boys were mine! As soon as she left that morning, I explained thoroughly the rules and regulations for keeping at least a modicum of household up-keep during the time of her absence.

Any snacks, trash, or eating utensils left in the TV room resulted in being barred from viewing TV with food items. Concerning dishes, the enforced rule was "you make it dirty, you make it clean!" Since Terry has taught them how to do laundry, dirty clothes left on the floor anywhere in the house will be thrown in the trash. They were on call to complete any chore I deemed necessary for the aseptic quality of our living quarters.

Part of the reason for these expectations was because I missed Terry, and, when she came home, I did not want her to fall into an immediate ill humor because of a messy house. Otherwise, my anticipation for a happy reunion could have been marred. Fellowship could have been seriously hindered if the house would have been found in a dysfunctional state of affairs.

Unsupervised males are prone to wrecking an interior's décor to the chagrin of most females.

However, the main reason for such scrutiny with the sons was because I did not want to have to deal personally with the mess. I did not want such concerns coming back on me. I despise laundry upkeep. I detest doing dishes. Housework just ain't my bag! Thus, I was motivated to maintain an efficient oversight.

Does it not make sense to you that, if one wants to keep the peace and does not want to deal with messy outcomes, careful diligence should be the order of every day?

Should not the same consideration be given to spiritual concerns as well?

For example, the Christian privilege of life in Christ bears with it the responsibility to live in a way which is pleasing to God. The deep, rich blessings of God are uniquely associated with the principles of Christian lifestyle.

Yet, it is an unfortunate reality that, so many who profess to have personal relationship with Christ, show themselves to be so careless and irresponsible with spiritual expectations.

There are two matters that God's people so often forget. First, if spiritual uncleanness is allowed to persist in our lives, fellowship with God is hindered. Second, spiritual dirt remaining unchecked creates messes, and messes bring unfortunate consequences.

I tell you what—one of the reasons I strive to stay away from sinful practices is because I do not want to have to deal the mess that will most certainly be created.

The bottom line is that we need to be diligent daily in the oversight of keeping our spiritual house clean. "Abide in Him that we be not ashamed."

One morning I found a partial pack of crackers in the TV room. The hammer has got to surely fall—snicker, snicker, snicker!

GET WEARY OF YOUR STRUGGLES, AND JUST GIVE IN

Do you ever get weary of struggling with personal, spiritual, and emotional issues, and just want to give in? Well, why don't you? After all, constantly struggling with concerns is very draining as well as unproductive to one's experience in life. The sooner one gives up struggling the sooner the relief.

If you are wondering if there is any real validity to this suggestion, consider the following.

One Sunday night I came home after church absolutely whipped. I was ready to wind down from the preaching, teaching, and counseling involved with the day. Honestly, I did not want to have to deal anything else.

But, my wife, Terry, met me at the front door, and said, "Keithen and Eran are fighting again. You are going to have to break it up." Times were when these two fought, and I had to crack down on them for being so combative.

My initial response was why she had not taken care of it. I mumbled grumpily at her as I went to check out the situation.

Both boys were lying on their bedroom floor. As tempers had flared, Keithen had stuck Eran into a very painful wrestling hold called the banana split. Keithen was mad and really cranking hard on it as he demanded Eran to apologize. Eran was mad, and, though squealing from the pain, was as defiant as he could be. They had been struggling in that position for at least fifteen minutes, but both were too proud to give in to the struggle.

I took one look, and walked out without saying a word. I went to my own downstairs bedroom, and dressed down. Terry followed thereafter, and we had a lengthy and somewhat heated discussion about the two brothers.

Twenty minutes later, I went and found them in the same angry position, but obviously very weary from the extended ordeal.

I got down right to Eran's ear, and calmly said, "Eran, I am going to make Keithen let go of you, and I do not want you to do or say anything to him."

I next got right up to Keithen's face, and told him gently, "Let your brother go."

Keithen willingly complied. Eran untangled his body from Keithen's. Both rose and went to their separate places without further incident.

What gets me is that they had to have someone to tell them to end their struggle. Both admitted a couple years later that they were so happy when I asked them to end it. It could have ended long before had they been willing to give in.

But, all of this leads to a very personal application to the grand scale of what transpires in our lives.

With what, or whom, are you struggling? It is quite clear that we live in a society in which many people are struggling in a variety of ways.

However, has it occurred to you that the single best option for every struggle is to quickly weary of it, and just give in? It is absolutely the right thing to do when one understands the purposeful exhortation and permission to do so by the Lord Jesus Christ.

Consider His words, "Come unto me, all ye that labor and are heavy laden, and I will give you rest." Why suffer in a pinning position when you can have release and relief?

Struggling, laboring, and laden people can have rest in the Lord as they quit and give in to His workable principles. It is really a rather simple prospect when one is willing to practice it. You will, most certainly, be less stressed and pressed.

Incidentally, I hope my boys are as smart with their children as I have been with them!

STAY AT HOME!

On November 14th, 2003, the Wahama White Falcons played in the first round of the West Virginia state playoffs. Their opponent that particular game was Doddridge County High School.

Late in the third quarter, the Doddridge offense lined up in a formation that had the clear markings of running a play to the short side of the field along their sideline. Our son, Jeshua, who played outside linebacker on defense, was positioned on the opposite side.

When the ball was snapped, and the play started moving as expected, Jeshua sprinted from his position, and tackled the quarterback from behind for about a three-yard loss.

I tell you what—it looked good to me. I clapped my hands, and yelled, "Way to go, Jesh!" Excited stands-fans cheered, too, at the defensive play.

I happened to be standing directly behind the team's defensive coordinator, James Toth, at the time. While many were cheering because of what was viewed as a good play, Coach Toth, on the other hand, held his game-plan ground about the play.

He raised his hand as high as he could stretch with his index finger pointed to the ground, and started yelling, "Jeshua, stay at home! Stay at home!" When Jeshua realized his name was being called, Coach Toth reiterated with the same gesture, "Son, stay at home! Stay at home!" Jeshua nodded knowingly.

It was then that I remembered. Jeshua had been reprimanded on a couple of occasions during the regular season for forsaking his contain position as an out-side linebacker. Coach Toth later explained how he could envision an opponent's offensive coordinator recognizing and exploiting such loss of contain for large rushing gains, which could, conceivably, make a difference in a game.

I have always instructed our boys to do what the coaches say to do, and be where the coaches want them to be. Jeshua's play, although appearing acceptable, was, in fact, a play that thwarted the coach's prescribed design. So, I felt a little sheepish for applauding the play.

This, however, makes for a powerful spiritual consideration.

Primarily, it reminds us how easy it is to fall into affirming moral behavior that runs contrary to the revealed will of God. For example, we unwittingly glo-rify couples who birth children outside of the marriage institution. We make heroes out of people who ingest vast quantities of beer. We acquiesce to the peer pressure to tolerate ungodly sexual practice. We comfort those who have to divorce because they just do not feel like working out their differences.

If you do not think it is true, make an honest evaluation of what is in the print media. Honestly evaluate TV commercials. Honestly evaluate public opinion. We are, oh, most certainly, cheering on in many ways that which may appear acceptable to humanistic reasoning, but is unacceptable to the standard of God's expectations.

All the while, God in Heaven is raising His hand, and pointing down to the Cross of Jesus Christ. He is holding the moral game-plan ground He has stipu-lated, and is calling to those who will listen, "Stay at home! Stay at home!"

It is critical for parents to "stay at home." It is imperative for churches to "stay at home." It is compulsory for society to "stay at home."

We are being grossly remiss for cheering on those who forsake positions of moral contain. The more we affirm it, the more it encourages others to forsake it.

All the while, Satan recognizes it, and is making some incredible end runs for significant societal and spiritual gains.

Coach Cromley later said he was also telling Jeshua the same thing. Our son, Ron, who is defensive coordinator at Musselman High School, gave similar reprimand after the game. Ah—such is the mindset of coaches.

3

GOD GIVES GREAT COMFORT

"BLESSED BE GOD, EVEN THE FATHER OF OUR LORD JESUS CHRIST, THE FATHER OF MERCIES, AND THE GOD OF ALL COMFORT; WHO COMFORTETH US IN ALL OUR TRIBULATIONS."

—(II CORINTHIANS: 3-4)

"AND, LORD, HELP LAURA HAVE A GOOD TIME IN HEAVEN."

Laura. She died so suddenly.

She died so young. Her ten years were too brief.

Laura's untimely death touched our community to the very core our being. The winter of 1994 was hard to endure. Her death made it more difficult.

When I carried Laura in my arms and placed her in the van for the arduous drive to the hospital, I never gave any consideration that this vivacious child was at that moment in the grip of a deadly illness to which she would succumb in the early morning hours.

And, of course, neither did Laura. Throughout the ordeal, she sought continuous re-assurance from her mother that I was still around to take them home.

It was distressing that Laura died. It was distressing because she was loved so much by her family. It was distressing because she was of immense value to the wholesome and earthy quality of our community landscape.

Jeshua was seven years old at the time of her death. He was very tender about it all. With tears cascading down his checks one evening, he climbed up in my lap and said, "Dad, I miss her."

The next morning during our family devotion time before school, Jeshua was asked to pray our prayer for us. He concluded his prayer with, "And, Lord, help Laura to have a good time in Heaven! Amen."

Jeshua's child-like prayer strengthened my soul. By it there was underscored a dynamic principle found only in faith and trust in Jesus Christ.

FOR, HOW NEEDFUL AND HOW POWERFUL IS THE HOPE OF HEAVEN!

The hope of Heaven instilled hope in the heart of a child. The hope of Heaven soothes the pain of a grieving Christian. The hope of Heaven helps us to see beyond the cold and dark barrier of death.

And, for a minister who feels with and for people, the hope of Heaven dilutes the poison of cynicism which can effectively annihilate a sense of the abundant qualities of life spoken of by our Savior.

According to Scripture, Heaven is a far better place.

Heaven is a large place with jeweled walls, jeweled foundations, and jeweled gates (Revelation 21).

Heaven is a place of life, light, and liberty (Revelation 22).

And, most important of all, Heaven is where Jesus Christ is (Revelation 21 & 22)! Thank God for Jesus Christ who lives and makes this hope possible through faith in His name. Without the hope of Heaven, we would be people most miserable (I Corinthians 15:19)!

Death touches us all at some point. Other parents experience the deaths of their young children. Such eventually came to our family. Every day, death overcomes people dear and precious to us.

But, by His own sacrifice and resurrection, Jesus Christ provides for each that receives Him the sure hope of Heaven!

I believe that God is indeed helping Laura to have a good time in Heaven!

As to Laura, we said good-bye. But, just for a short time. For, our own hope of heaven will be realized someday, because Jesus will be there to take us home, too.

<u>SEIZURE!</u>

When I left the house to officiate a basketball game January 11th, 1999, Jamin, four years-old at the time, was asleep on the couch.

In the second quarter of the game, my partner cracked his whistle, and I turned to see him talking to a policeman. Beckoning me to the sideline, the policeman informed me that Jamin had become ill, and that he was being taken by ambulance to Pleasant Valley Hospital.

Later, I learned that Jamin experienced a seizure just shortly after waking up. What a frightening experience it was for Terry and the boys to see him seize. I got Jeshua's and Micaiah's version when I got home later that night. "It was the most awful thing I have ever seen," said our 11-year old, Jeshua. Our six-year old, Micaiah, explained that he tried to keep everybody calm! Mom had a little different account about our Mr. Micaiah during those tense moments in the Branch house. But, overall, the three of them handled the situation very well.

It was almost unreal to me what I heard that good policeman say about my son. In those moments, I experienced seizure, too.

First, I experienced the seizure of spiritual prayer. While standing out on that gym floor surrounded by basketball players and the noise of people in the stands, I prayed in the Holy Spirit. How is that possible, you ask? You think that such talk sounds radical? Romans 8:26 assures us, "Likewise the Spirit also helpeth our infirmities: for we know not what we should pray for as we ought: but the Spirit Himself maketh intercession for us." The Holy Spirit knew how disadvantaged I was. With His help in those moments, confusion was eliminated and direction given. It is far better to be seized in prayer by Him than to react on a whim.

Second, I experienced the seizure of implicit trust in God for the life and health of my family. That type of seizure provided a sense of sedation to my soul, for, in times like that, the mind is capable of imagining all manner of useless scenarios, which stimulate unnecessary stress and anxiety. Yes, I understood clearly what was communicated to me. There had been an emergency situation at home. One of my sons was ill for some reason that warranted the work of the rescue squad. But, you can't beat it with a stick when God grabs your heart and mind, and says, "Trust me." "And the peace of God, which passeth all understanding, shall keep your hearts and minds through Christ Jesus" (Philippians 4:7).

Third, I experienced the seizure of complete confidence in my beloved wife, Terry. There was nothing that I could do where I was, which eliminated the option to worry. Regardless of what was happening, it was assuring to know that she was there. The two of us are a team. We understand our responsibility as parents, and are both committed to the fulfillment of that responsibility. Has it occurred to you the incredible importance God places upon loving and cooperative spouses in the building of strong, secure families? What is the inestimable value in the home when spouses have exceeding confidence in each other?

Furthermore, I experienced the seizure of support from my church family. Beth Pierce arrived quickly at the house to care for the boys. My deacons rallied at the hospital to support us while we were still in the emergency room. It was amazing how quickly they arrived to minister to their pastor and his family. The next day Jamin received a multitude of balloons, and a variety of toys and coloring books from the people of the church to occupy his mind during his hospital stay. I work hard to minister to the church in which God has entrusted to me, but during a tense night and taxing day, the church family represented God to their pastor and family. I really do not know how people get by without having a strong attachment to a loving church family.

Yet, all of this is related purposely. It is not to uplift our crisis, or to build up my wife, or to brag on the church I pastor. Rather, it is to communicate to you the powerful assistance facilitated by Godly relationships during crises.

You see, God's Word makes it clear—sometimes bad things happen to God's people. The bad things that happen are not God's fault. But, when they do, it is far better to experience the seizure of Godly relationships which minimize the seizures of defeat, dejection, and doubt that can seize and jerk our lives into crumpled threads.

Check out the Scripture. How comforting to Jesus was it that, during His crisis on the Cross, He could commend the care of His mother, Mary, to Apostle John? How motivating was it to Paul during some of his crises that the Philippian church cared for and supported him? How meaningful was it to David in his crisis that he had a faithful friend in Jonathan? How inspiring to the people in the Book of Hebrews was it to be reminded about the assurance of God, "I will never leave thee, nor forsake thee." How important is it for you to prepare to experience the seizure of Godly relationships during crises that most assuredly will come and seize you?

"Dad," asked Jamin as he punched a bunch of balloons.

"Yes, son."

"Did I have a seizure?"

"You sure did," I replied. And, with thanks in my heart to God, I added, "And, I did, too."

IT HURTS WHERE?

Each of our three home sons played 2004 football on different levels, which meant Terry and I attended three football games a week.

This is not quite as rigorous as it was during the 1997 season when we attended four games a week involving our boys. Eran's junior high games were on Thursdays, Keithen's high school varsity games were on Fridays, Ron's games with Shepherd College were on Saturdays, and Jeshua's peewee games were on Sunday afternoons.

I felt like I was the most blessed man in the whole wide world!

Micaiah's junior high practice was in its second week, and it surprised me how he complained about being so sore. Of all our boys, he is the one who has most taken it upon his self to maintain good athletic condition during times when he is not specifically involved in playing a sport.

As a matter of fact, after arriving home one Monday evening from practice, he groaned to his mother, "I am so sore from our football practices that the inside of my butt hurts!"

When Terry told me what he had said, I needed a verbal retake. I asked, "It hurts where?"

It is clear that an athlete's muscles get sore when pre-season drills start. We can empathize with them when they moan about sore shoulder muscles, for example, because we have had sore shoulder muscles ourselves. We may even voluntarily apply some massage to help ease the discomfort because, knowing where they hurt, we know how they hurt.

But, Micaiah's description of soreness because of football practice is beyond me. I find it quite abstruse that he could hurt in the manner which he described.

By way of contrast, there are many types of hurts that are not related to physical stresses and strains. These are rather associated with the unfortunate hurts of the heart and the emotion.

Sometimes people try to put their hurts into perspective so that others may understand and be better able to offer some needed comfort. But, all too often others respond with the attitude of, "It hurts where? It hurts how?" They prove to be miserable comforters because they themselves have never hurt in the manner described.

Such was the experience of a man in the Bible named Job, who suddenly experienced a season of great distress. In short work, he learned that all ten of his children had been killed, his financial holdings were destroyed, and his sterling reputation was maligned.

Three friends visited with Job, but they proved to be utter failures when it came to ministering to Job. They could not empathize, and, therefore, could not console.

At one point, Job blurted, "Miserable comforters are you all."

While all of us have at some point felt no one understands our hurts, it is a surety that God always does. For example, the Psalmist was sure of this vital spiritual truth when he verified about the Lord, "Like as a father pities his children, so the Lord pities them that fear Him, for He knows our frame."

In other words, God knows us inside-and-out to the point that He is able to comfort us whenever we hurt and wherever we hurt. Speaking through Isaiah, God affirms, "When you pass through the waters, through the rivers, or through the fires, I will be with you."

You may be experiencing hurt in such a way that no one seems to understand or have any interest. But, our Heavenly Father, because of His love for you, is very much aware of it. "Cast your care upon Him, for He cares for you."

In the meantime, I jokingly suggested Preparation-H to Micaiah, but I do not think he saw the humor in it.

4

GOD EMPHASIZES THE PRIORITY OF THE CHURCH

○ ○

"HIS HABITATION SHALL YE SEEK, AND THITHER THOU SHALT COME"

—(DEUTERONOMY 12:5)

"NOT FORSAKING THE ASSEMBLING OF OURSELVES TOGETHER"

—(HEBREWS 10:25)

THE SUNDAY RUSH
(Written by Keithen Branch for one of his classes at Ohio Northern Univesity)

"Everything in the house is quiet and still as the darkness reluctantly releases its choking grip on the sun. As the twilight invades our repose, I become faintly aware of the thumping footsteps of my father as he rises from his bed to start Sunday morning.

"Dad is always the first to awake from his dreams. He is a man of large stature that pastors a local church, preaching with stereotypical ranting and raving to accompany his pacing to-and-fro. It all produces a facial red-glow as he shouts down a fire-and-brimstone message.

"Early to church, he leaves behind his family to join him hours later. But, little does he realize the adventure that takes place every Sunday morning after he has left.

"Later, Mom is the next to awake. Then, it is on to us brothers. You can hear her go from room to room, knocking on each door, and sweetly uttering gentle words to get us up. Her greeting is with tender gestures laced with such love only a mother can offer her children. Hearing Mom's voice is a wonderful way to wake up.

"Departing to finish her own preparation, she fully expects us to rise and prepare for the approaching service.

"Minutes later, however, she makes a second pass, and finds that all of us are still sleeping. Once again, she utters sweet words trying to motivate us to cast off our warm blankets and prepare for church.

"After she leaves, we fall asleep again. But, when she returns for a third time, she is not the same person that gently aroused previously. Now, she is very agitated, and offers many threats of alternative actions if we do not get our butts out of bed. Fearing for our young lives, we emerge from our rooms in a mad dash to begin the church-preparation ritual.

"Thus begins the adventure of the Sunday rush. Our rebellious inactivity has stirred our mother, and it is straight downhill from there.

"I try to be a mature example for my brothers as I rise quickly and prepare. But, it also gives me a vantage to view my brothers in action, for it is amazing how they flaunt our mother.

"For example, she has set forth the rule of no cartoons before church. Yet, it is contemptible how they sneak through the house in a covert attempt to catch a glimpse of their favorite toon—that is, until Mom catches them. Each discovery makes her more irate, and the threats become more severe.

"Furthermore, it is contemptible how the little boogers get dressed. It seems they always find their favorite pants with the hole in the knee, or the T-shirt with multitudinous stains. They purposely refuse to wear anything else.

"Mom's threats become actions. A rump swat or two gets them to see it her way.

"I listen and laugh as they grumble through their sniffles that their choice of clothing was fine. They always say they wore those clothes last week to church, which, of course, is never the case.

"Mom gave up on cooking Sunday breakfast a long time ago. We all try to grab a Pop Tart on the way out because it seems like we are always on the threshold of being late for church.

"Along the way, Mom attempts to restore herself to beauty. The Sunday Rush always leaves her disheveled.

"At church, we proceed inside and greet the members. We worship God, and have a wonderful time doing so. Dad preaches his customary lively message, and we go home. The heated adventure of the morning is long forgotten. The next week, we will do the same thing again."

Is it like this at your house, too? The Psalmist who said "I was glad when they said unto me, Let us go unto the House of the Lord," must not have had children.

Nonetheless, regardless of what takes to get your family and you to church, just get there!

"MY TEAM NEEDS ME!"

If there is one thing that I notice about our three younger sons, it is that they understand their importance to their respective baseball teams. We teach our boys the ideal of team. Play the best you can and contribute as much as possible to the team's goal of winning. Team comes first.

But, I suppose children get the ideal distorted at times.

Once, our older son, Keithen, took our five year old, Jamin, swimming in a church members pool. Keithen instructed Jamin that he needed to be careful while they swam.

"Jamin, you have got to listen to me at all times," Keithen said.

"Okie dokie," Jamin replied. Most of the time the younger brothers are submissive to the older brothers only when it is to their distinct advantage.

"You are not supposed to run around the pool either."

"I know. I know."

"And you will have to wear one their lifejackets, too."

"Why?"

"It is for your safety. We want to make sure that you do not drown."

Jamin was briefly silent as he apparently contemplated the ramifications of his possible drowning.

"Yeah. It wouldn't be good for me to drown," he philosophically responded.

Keithen chuckled. "Why is that, Jamin?"

"Because—my baseball team needs me!"

I was somewhat dumbfounded when Keithen told me how Jamin had responded. In Jamin's perspective, it was not a matter whether his Mom, Dad, or brothers needed him. Rather, it was because his T-ball baseball team needed him.

Have I made a parental error somewhere along the line?

Jamin's concept does have a logical point when considered from a spiritual perspective. As we broaden the scope of his statement, we can add with great conviction that as a born-again Christian, you have a team that needs you, too!

Specifically, the Scripture points out to us that believers in the Lord Jesus Christ are a part of the body of Christ. "Now ye are the body of Christ, and members in particular."

This Scriptural truth is played out rather poignantly within Christ's establishment of the local church. It is within the context of the local church and its membership that Christians come together for worship, evangelism, and ministry.

Furthermore, the family concept is very applicable to the local church because believers have been made a part of God's family.

But, the team concept should be considered, too. If the local church is to be fruitful, then its members need to be active and faithful. Its members need to cooperate and contribute.

Furthermore, if something happens to one of the members of the local church, it affects the whole church. "And whether one member suffer, all the members suffer with it; or one member be honored, all the members rejoice with it."

It follows that if a member is ill, it affects the whole church body. If a member falls into grievous sin, or does not edify the church with their spiritual gift, or is not faithful to worship, it affects the whole church body.

Scripturally, every Christian should be a member of a local church. Church membership is a privilege in which every member is just as important as the other. "And the eye cannot say unto the hand, I have not need of thee: nor again the head to the feet, I have no need of you."

But, sadly, many treat church membership with carelessness and disdain.

We all need to remember that our church team needs us.

The next time you want to lay out of church, remember the words of a child, "My team needs me!"

HUNGRY!

Yes, I know—boys will be boys.

But, the Preacher's boys misbehave at church, too, many times to my chagrin. Though we have after-church meetings at home concerning it, at-church behavior sometimes does not improve immediately.

For example, one Sunday afternoon, we had to leave church quickly for a 60-mile trip to make a 2 PM meeting.

Before going to church that morning, Terry prepared drinks and sandwiches for us to eat while traveling. Jamin, our husky one and 5-year old at the time, was hungry again by the time he arrived at church for Sunday School. He was told that he would have to wait until after church before he could eat his sandwiches. He demonstrated the expected huff-and-puff.

During worship, I preached a four-pointer about the Holy Spirit from Acts 2, and extended the invitation, to which several responded.

On the second verse of the invitation hymn, Jamin left the side of his mother, who had her eyes closed and head bowed in prayer, and began to walk toward the back of the church.

I thought to myself, "Now, where does that boy think he's going? He knows better than this."

Toward the back, he entered a pew, and stood for a moment, then he exited and entered the pew behind. The next thing I knew, he just walked right out of the church!

I was flabbergasted and bumfuzzled in the pulpit.

I refrained from bellowing, "Boy, where do you think your are going?" I started to go say something to Terry about it, but another person came to the altar about that time, and I went to pray alongside of them.

By the time I got to the car after the service, the family was eating. Jamin was already chewing on his third sandwich. That boy sure likes to eat.

But, I was irritated at him, and, as soon as we were out of the church parking lot, I started the scolding process.

Driving through our town of Mason, WV, I scolded about inappropriate behavior in God's house.

Across the bridge over the Ohio River, I emphasized the importance of reverence during the invitation part of the worship service.

By the time we got into the cross-river town of Pomeroy, Ohio, I had vented an adequate portion of exasperation, and it finally occurred to me to ask, "Jamin, I just want to know why in this whole wide world you sneaked away from your mother and left the church?"

Sometimes parents get so worked up over their kid's actions that they forget to ask the obvious questions.

He replied meekly, "So I could get to the car first before Micaiah and Jeshua."

"Great time of day, boy! Why did you have to get to the car first?"

There was a pause. The question obviously embarrassed him. I adjusted the rearview mirror so I could see him.

He had his head bowed. His little lips quivered. He loosely held a sandwich part in one hand, and a pop can in the other hand.

Finally, he answered lowly, "'Cause—cause I was hungry...."

Terry and I looked at each other. In a half-whisper, struggling to suppress bubbling laughter, I leaned slightly toward her, and said, "He said he left because he was hungry."

It struck me as absolutely funny that our five-year old had been so intent on beating his brothers to the car to be the first one to the food. We snickered the rest of the way through Pomeroy.

But, the boy has demonstrated in a biting way a serious spiritual circumstance, which is so typical of many people. Jamin was willing to leave the worship service because he was hungry.

Without question, people are hungry today. However, their hunger is representative of a grave spiritual shortcoming, for they are not hungry for the things that matter most.

Food is not necessarily the focus here. Rather, the pivotal point concerns people who are hungry for personal pleasure and sensual satisfaction to the exclusion of experience with God. Philippians 3:19 explains that the god of today is the "belly." A vast portion of people is driven by what the self wants.

Furthermore, the hunger pains for gratification direct decisions and dominate choices. The Scripture accurately portrays the people of these last days as "lovers of pleasure more than lovers of God" (II Timothy 3:4). For all that is available, the hunger people have for the flesh-pots of the world never bring a lasting satisfaction to living.

What has happened to being hungry for God? Jesus said, "Blessed they which do hunger and thirst after righteousness: for they shall be filled" (Matthew 5:6).Our contemporary society is severely, spiritually short because there is little hunger for Almighty God.

"Wherefore do ye spend money for that which is not bread? And your labor for that which satisfied not? Hearken diligently unto me, and eat ye that which is good, and let your soul delight itself in fatness" (Isaiah 55:2).

Man's innate hunger will never be satisfied until we belly up to God's table and feed on His fine fare.

Fellowship with Him is filling.

Serving Him is satisfying.

Life in Him is the best of living.

"The meek shall eat and be satisfied: they shall praise the Lord that seek Him: your heart shall live forever" (Psalms 22:26).

Are you hungry? Be patient, and let God fix you a good meal.

YOU CAN SLIDE ON YOUR BUTT ONLY SO FAR

Our two youngest boys once played summer baseball on the same team for the Mason Bulldogs in the 9-10 years old minor league. Though the six-inning games of players this age are often time marathons, their play is spiced with enough humor to keep spectators sufficiently alert.

In a game involving our team and the Syracuse Reds, a young man, Chance Reed, worked the plate, and Jeshua, our 15-year old, and I called the bases.

Jamin was on first base when the following batter laced a base hit to left field. Jamin advanced to second, but when the throw went to the catcher, Jamin started chugging for third.

Though Jeshua moved into position for a possible call, I could tell that Jamin could make the base easily. Nonetheless, the Reds' catcher fielded the ball, and hastened to make a throw for a putout attempt. The third baseman stood excitedly in front of the bag.

Coach Sam Thompson yelled loudly to Jamin, "You're up," which meant no slide was necessary. But, from about three feet from the bag, Jamin started into a slide for the bag. When his butt hit the ground, it slid just a few inches. It seemed as though it got stuck to the dirt.

So, there he was with his leg stuck straight-out, and his foot about six inches from the bag. He was straining his foot out as far as he could in an effort to touch the base.

In the meantime, the third baseman received the throw. But, in the excitement of the moment, he was not quite sure what he needed to do.

While Jamin was straining and stretching toward the bag, the boy at third danced all over the bag with the ball in his glove.

While one coach yelled "Tag him," the other yelled "Get on the bag!" Such is the type of baseball drama often displayed on this level of play.

However, by way of contemplative comparison, it rather reveals an uncanny characteristic indicative of the Christian church at large. It is the unfortunate, contemporary spiritual condition of the church of being in a sliding mode with apparently little realization that it can slide only so far on its butt.

The spiritual life of any church suffers when its membership thinks that it can slide all the way around the spiritual bases of Christian responsibility. Eventually, the cumulative effect of the butt on the ground for too long will result in coming short of reaching the next bag.

Besides, God did not design the church for sliding. Rather, He calls to the church, "You're up!"

First, God designed the church to stand—not to slide. There is definitive action exhibited in God's expectation for the church to stand. We are called to stand fast, to stand in the faith, and to stand in His freedom. We are called to stand in the Spirit, and to stand with the Savior.

Second, God designed the church to walk—not to slide. "Walk" refers to the course that the Christian is expected to pursue to obtain the objectives of God.

Third, God designed the church to run—not to slide. "Run with patience the race set before us," the Scripture says, which speaks of endurance and strength that should be characteristic of all saved by Christ.

The church must not and cannot be content with a sliding attitude or perspective toward the redemptive plans of God. Sliding puts us on our butts, and it puts a real drag to forward motion when the butt is in contact with the ground.

It is only by standing, walking, and running that we position ourselves for touching all the bases from the great hit Jesus made on Calvary, the place that became the arena of man's struggle for spiritual and eternal survival.

It was there that Christ hit Satan's slider of sin, knocking the Adversary off the mound. The Savior's slam deserves decisive movement around the bases of spiritual responsibility rather than feeble slides on our butts.

Jamin finally got the situation figured out before being tagged out by the third baseman.

Jamin merely rolled over onto his belly, and touched the base with his hand!

A SNICKERS IN THE SNOW IS A SIGN FOR THE SAVED!

Several years ago on a cold, snowy Sunday, I taught a certain children's message during worship service about dealing with problems through the power and might of God. When I displayed a Snickers candy bar, the eyes of the kids widened, and several expressed a keen interest in having it for themselves.

I told the children that the Snickers Bar represented the sweetness and goodness of life that comes from God, which we all want to experience. However, many times problems in life seem to hinder us from having it.

To prove the point, I told them we were going to have a little contest. In the next few moments, one of the children won the prize. The others were very disappointed until I pulled out a bag of bars, and told them that after church each would receive one.

I asked for a volunteer to close the children's message with prayer. Our son, Jeshua, who was six years old at the time, said the prayer, which went like this, "Lord, PAL-E-E-S-E make sure that my Daddy lets us have our Snickers Bar after church! Amen!" The whole church burst out in laughter. They figured that Jeshua did not trust his dad to hold the bag without sampling some for himself.

The children indeed received their Snickers, but it is what Jeshua did with his own bar after church that sets the stage for a keen spiritual truth. Little did we know how concerned he was about whether he would get to eat his treat or not. Apparently, there were some serious considerations, which posed as potential problems to him.

First, he considered his family circumstances. He had three older brothers who often tried to bully him. Also, he was aware that his younger brother seemed to get his way all too often just to stop his whining. Then there was Mom, who simply loves Snickers bars. What will happen if I go home with this candy bar, he reasoned? Everybody would want a piece, and there would not be much left for himself.

Second, he considered putting the bar into his pocket, but he knew that a chocolate candy bar would certainly melt in that type of warm enclosure.

So, he came up with a unique solution. He went outside into the churchyard and furtively stuck his Snickers bar into a pile of snow! He fully expected it to be there and edible when he went back for it.

That evening when we returned to church, I just happened to see him retrieve it, peel off the wrapper, and eat it with delight. The sweetness and goodness of it had been perfectly preserved for its intended purpose at the most advantageous moment for him.

But, as I laughed and entered the church, a powerful spiritual truth began to emerge in my heart. It began to occur to me how the Snickers in the snow is a sign for the saved!

Recall Jeremiah 13 and the Sign of the Marred Linen Girdle. God told Jeremiah to put on a girdle, which was a type of belt. After wearing it a while, God next instructed him to take the belt and place it in a hole along the Euphrates River. Sometime later, Jeremiah was told to retrieve the girdle, and when he did, Jeremiah found that the girdle had become dry-rotted. It had become useless. It had become "profitable for nothing" (Jeremiah 13:7).

By having Jeremiah do this, God was painting a poignant picture of spiritual truth before the eyes of His people with that moldy, old belt Jeremiah had worn. The girdle was symbolic of Israel wrapped around God for a divine purpose. Israel was supposed to be a "people, a name, a praise, and a glory" to God (Jeremiah 13:11). But, Israel had permitted herself to become stuck in the holes of pride and worldly influence to the point of spiritual dry rot. God said they that had become "as this girdle, which is good for nothing" (Jeremiah 13:10).

The prophetic analogy was very condemning then, and the contemporary comparison is obvious now. Self-pride and worldly influence have ruined the testimony of many professing Christians. Spiritual mildew and dry-rot have become pervasive within the ranks of the church.

God then asks a very forthright question in relation to it all, "Can the Ethiopian change his skin, or the leopard his spots? Then can you do good who are accustomed to doing evil" (Jeremiah 13:23).

The point is that sometimes people get so used to doing evil that change becomes an impossibility! As far as God is concerned, they become profitable and good for nothing!

Just how sad would it be for a person to get to that point in life? Your life is supposed to be wrapped around God, and not around the things of the world.

The church is supposed to be wrapped around God, and not around the things of the world. The world has too much of a rotting effect.

When Jeshua went to retrieve that Snickers bar from that pile of snow, he fully expected that its sweetness and goodness would be preserved for his enjoyment.

Consider, by contrast, that, since God has saved us and redeemed us with the expensive price of Jesus' blood, he, too, should expect us to preserve in ourselves the sweetness and goodness of life that is found in holy and sanctified living.

The Christian who becomes marred by self-pride and worldly influence is a disappointment to God and will be judged. "Hear ye, and give ear; be not proud: for the Lord hath spoken" (Jeremiah 13:15).

Just like the day when Jeremiah pulled that belt out of the hole, the Snickers in the snow pulled out by Jeshua is a powerful reminder of what God expects from His people.

DON'T MOVE THAT LANDMARK!

Once when Micaiah was in the hospital grievously ill, I had the home duties. Making room rounds to get the boys up for school one morning, I made a dreaded discovery. The water tank on a commode was leaking (pardon the pun) liberally onto the floor, which was sopping wet.

Since there was no stop-valve, I drained (no pun intended) the tank, and propped a short crowbar in such a way as to hold the water valve closed.

The three older boys emerged from their rooms, and I explained why not to use that particular bathroom. But, because of getting busy with other morning preparations, I did not get it explained to Jeshua, the six year-old at the time.

Later, I got out my Bible to prepare for morning devotions. I did not think too much about it when I heard a "squeeeeeeshsh." I heard it a second time—"squeeeeeeshsh." And, a third time—"squeeeeeeeshshsh."

Suddenly, I realized what it was, as well as who it was. I rushed to the bathroom where I saw Jeshua sitting backward on the pot in his underwear. He was having a big time manipulating the water valve with that crowbar, which made more water available in the tank to tinkle onto the floor.

"Oh, no, Son! Leave it alone. I have that crowbar there for a purpose!"

Hold that thought for a moment, because, indeed, many things are set where they are for a definite purpose.

From the Scripture, we read that, as God's people became established in the land of promise, each Hebrew family received a certain portion of property. Since maps or deeds of property were little used, various types of markers were used to designate the property lines. Landmarks were placed where they were for a definite purpose.

Thus, one of the holy instructions from God involved warning to not move the landmarks. A moved landmark was deceitful and harmful.

The gravity of not moving landmarks is just as relevant today as it was then. As a matter of fact, it is a critical point for each of us to consider from God's holy perspective.

Undoubtedly, God has established some needed individual and corporate landmarks for beneficent purposes, and it is important that we do not move them.

For example, we should be cautioned to not move that landmark of potential and possibilities God has set in our lives.

Deuteronomy 19:14 states to not move the "landmark which they of old have set in thine inheritance, which thou shalt inherit."

It is sure that each of us has tremendous potential, which could lead to powerful possibilities. God has set the mark of a great inheritance for our lives in terms of rich blessing, temporal accomplishment, and spiritual victory.

But, too many move their God-given landmarks. With poor attitudes, with God-less decisions, and with un-Christ-like actions, we move our landmarks. The unfortunate result is that we wind up moving our landmarks inward, which closes to the gap of possibilities.

Furthermore, we should take care to not move the landmark of God's influence on secular life. "Remove not the ancient landmarks, which thy fathers have set."

Has it occurred to you that it was God through our nation's founding fathers that set the landmark of Christian principles to affect the moral tone in America? Yet, there is a great effort going on by societal elitists to remove the spiritual landmarks of God.

It is everything right, good, and essential that the spiritual landmarks God set for America remain unmoved!

Otherwise, it will be like us sitting backward on a commode pot playing with the water, only to have it leak out and soak us with the consequences.

Squeeeeeshsh!

SELF-CENTEREDNESS IS BEING BY FAR TOO NEAR-SIGHTED

Over the years, our sons have demonstrated attitudes of fierce competition among themselves as it has concerned athletic prowess. Competition among siblings for varieties of reasons is often typical in families. Most of inter-family competitiveness stems from that egotism to have primacy in the family pecking order. At least, such has seemed to be the emotional concern in the Branch family of six boys from their parent's perspective.

For example consider Micaiah and Jamin who are involved in the sport of wrestling. After practices, one or the other invariably comes home cocky because he beat his brother in practice, and the other is down in the dumps because he lost to his brother in practice. The loser has the usual frowny-faced, whinny-voiced explanation, "I LOST BECAUSE HE CHEATED!" The same at home whenever they break out into a wrestling match, or any other game for that matter.

Whenever we have gone to tournaments, these two seem more driven to win in their respective age and weight classes because each wants to outshine the other.

However, there is a wry irony manifested in each of these competitive brothers. When Jamin is on the mat wrestling an opponent, Micaiah is usually on hand cheering vigorously for Jamin. The same is true for Jamin when Micaiah is wrestling. I have seen both give little coaching clinics with advice and suggestions for the next match out of concern for each other.

At a certain pee wee wrestling tournament, Jamin did very well, but Micaiah struggled. When Micaiah lost a hard match, Jamin, to everyone's surprise, ran and got under the bleachers, and cried piteously. No one could get him to come out for a long time.

Later, Jamin asked, "Dad, when we get home, can I give Micaiah one of the little trophies I got last year so he can have one for today, too?"

As their Dad, concern for one another is gratifying to see in these two. They are not so self-centered that they cannot see the other.

It is with this thought that the Scripture stipulates a principle that bears on us considerably, for to be self-centered is by far being too near-sighted. When we only see ourselves and see no one else, our sight is definitely too narrow in scope.

Galatians 6:2 states, "Bear ye one another's burdens, and so fulfill the law of Christ."

Undoubtedly, we are living in very competitive times. Many people are living to be the best, and to get the best out of life. In many respects, we see a grasping ethic in society that is focused so much on self that others are neglected. "It is a dog-eat-dog world," we often intone. We uplift the winners, and ignore the losers.

But, there is a grave injustice on this type of perspective in life. The injustice is found in the emphasis on "me and mine." Society literally supports the concept that if it is not "me and mine," then everything else is an inconvenience. If something taps into personal resources, then there is great lament and deep sense of personal loss.

It is very easy to get caught up in this type of mindset. Yet, there is a great Christian principle which should be uplifted in the face of our "me and mine" society.

While it is right and good that we strive to excel within the context of God's will for our lives, it is far more virtuous to be mindful of others to the extent that at times we help them bear their burdens in life. This critical principle motivates us to not be so near-sighted with a self-centered focus.

God has so structured society that our lives are closely woven together. Therefore, we need one another. When we direct neglect or evil toward one another, we, in fact, hurt ourselves.

In what way, then, is it possible to practice this imperative Christian principle? The answer is clearly found in "the law of Christ."

This "law of Christ" may be stated and confirmed in several Scriptural ways, but the embodiment and fulfillment of this law is found in the facts of the Cross and Resurrection of Jesus Christ.

This is true, because, in dying on the Cross and rising from the dead, He considered us as important, and was willing to give of Himself. Through His plan of redemption, Jesus Christ bore the burden for our salvation. He bore the burden of our guilt for sin. He bore the burden for our having peace with God. He bore the burden that we might have life and life more abundantly.

The outgrowth of His redemptive acts is that He offers Himself as a partner to walk with us through life. He helps bear the burdens of our sorrows, our disappointments, and our tribulations. Jesus said, "Come unto me, all ye that labor and are heavy laden, and I will give you rest" (Matthew 11:28).

Jesus was never near-sighted with self-centeredness, for He made it perfectly clear, "The Son of man came not to be ministered unto, but to minister, and to give His life a ransom for many" (Matthew 20:28).

Exemplified by Christ, it is this very precept of concern for others and giving of self to others that often serve to lighten heavy loads that others bear. Stand ready with involved compassion and encouragement for the sake of others and the glory of God.

Micaiah asked Jamin why he cried. Jamin told him, "I wanted you to win, too."

Micaiah simply replied, "Thanks." Micaiah won his next match.

5

GOD'S SALVATION IS TOO GREAT TO BE NEGLECTED

○ ○

"HOW SHALL WE ESCAPE, IF WE NEGLECT SO GREAT SALVATION"

—(HEBREWS 2:3)

"HEY, DAD! YOU DON'T EVEN HAVE TO PAY FOR IT THIS TIME!"

Those of you who manage the money at home know how it is to deal with the persistent requests of your children. The general response usually goes something like this, "I don't have the money to pay for it this time." But, the rub is that you don't necessarily want your kids to let the neighbors know how financially uncooperative you have to be at times.

With our boys, I usually have to deal with eating-out requests, such as one request by Micaiah for some ice-cream at the Middleport Dairy Queen before one of his youth baseball games.

"Oh, I suppose I have the money to pay for it this time," I agreed. All the family was happy with Dad.

Near the end of the game, the father of our team's coach told me that his son planned to treat the boys at Dairy Queen because it was the final game of the season.

My heart smiled as I thought, "Ain't that nice!"

But, Micaiah soon obliterated my internal bubble with an accurate shot of embarrassment.

The coach gathered the boys around the mound after the game. And, from our vantage point, we could tell by the boy's reaction when the coach told them about the Dairy Queen treat.

Suddenly, however, Micaiah broke from the huddle with two joyful jumps. In the hearing of all, Micaiah yelled, "Hey, Dad! We're going to Dairy Queen! You don't even have to pay for it this time!"

People laughed at his words, because they knew exactly what he meant.

But, seconds later, my mind was brimming with moving thoughts about the import of Micaiah's words. So much around me reminds me about God. The things I see. The things I hear. As I trucked back to the van with Micaiah's words as inspiration, I whispered, "Thank you, God."

You see, when I consider the salvation of my boys, my wife, and myself, in addition to all else God does for our family, the truth is that I do not have to pay for it. God has already paid for it.

When we make request for Heaven, we do not have to pay for it, because God already has. When we make request for peace, we do not have to pay for it, because God already has. When we make request for eternal life, we do not have to pay for it, because God already has.

Someone somewhere always has to pay for what we have. Just like a child must look to his father or mother to pay for what they obtain, so we must look to our Heavenly Father if ever we are to obtain salvation and abundant life for today, hope for tomorrow, and certainty for the future.

The payment, however, is not found in the value which comes from dollars and cents. It has rather come in the form of personal sacrifice.

The Scripture is explicit about it. "For God so loved the world that He gave His only begotten Son." "For ye are bought with a price." "For as much as ye know that ye were not redeemed with corruptible things, as silver and gold, but with the precious blood of Christ."

Through His Son, Jesus Christ, God paid it all at Calvary on the Cross. He paid it all to change our eternal destination from hell to Heaven. He paid it all because we could not pay for it ourselves. The price He paid was so high that it prevails upon us to reciprocate with our own respectful and reverent commitment and dedication to Him.

"Hey, Dad! You don't even have to pay for it this time!"

Son, because of God, I don't have to pay for it at any time.

THAT'S MY SON'S BLOOD SMEARED ON THE DOOR!

The parking lot was vacant. The crowd, which had attended the Wednesday evening revival service, was gone. I was basking in the glow of the Holy Spirit because I was aware of several manifestations of His presence in the service just concluded.

As I ascended the basement steps, however, I heard the deep, hurting wails of three-year old Jamin. The outside door burst open. His little face appeared, and it was smeared with blood!

"I'm bleeding!" he cried. "I'm bleeding! I'm bleeding!"

He had fallen on the asphalt while running from one of his brothers. His nose was bleeding. A scrape on his forehead was bleeding. He had swiped blood all across the right side of his face.

The next morning I arrived at the church at 5 AM. As I walked up to the door, I noticed something unusual on it. Stooping in the darkness, I could not identify what it was. I turned on the outside light, and took another look.

Instantly, I knew what it was. It was from the previous night. It was blood! My son's blood was smeared on the door! I reeled in amazement as a powerful truth from God's Word crystallized in my mind.

Scripture records God's powerful deliverance of Israel from Egyptian bondage. God through Moses declared that on a certain night God would permit the Destroyer to kill every Egyptian first born.

However, Israel was told to take the blood of an atoning lamb, and to smear the blood over their doors. God said, "When I see the blood, I will pass over you!"

While Israel cringed at the mournful wails of a nation in the throes of death, Israel received the mercy of God because of blood smeared on their doors. By contrast, the Egyptians, without the protection of atoning blood, received biting judgment from God.

The bloody sight on our own church door captured for me a deeper insight to the experience of Israel as God passed those Hebrew homes with bloody doors.

Clearly, God did not see lamb's blood, but **THE LAMB'S BLOOD**—The Lamb of whose blood was shed before the foundation of the world for man's release from bondage to Sin. In God's eyes, that was the blood of His Son smeared on the doors!

I know assuredly that it moved God with compassion when He came to a bloodstained door. Oh, the compassion I felt for my son when I saw his blood on our church door. Oh, the greater and nobler compassion God has for us because of the blood of His Son atoning for our lives.

The preciousness of Jamin's blood on the door meant something to me. But, the preciousness of Jesus' blood means something for all.

On the church door of Willow Island Baptist Church was smeared the blood of my son, Jamin. But, on the heart-doors of the Church of the Redeemed is the blood of God's Son, Jesus.

I now know God's compassion for me and for us in a deeper way. And, I say, "Thank you, God!"

<u>GET UP!</u>

Our boys set a new record for Christmas morning, 2000. They came barreling into our bedroom at 2:54 AM.

We knew they would be up early. Every year previous it has been usually between four and five AM on Christmas morning. But, that particular Christmas we did not think it would wind up being six minutes before three. After all, we did not get home until 11:30, and into bed before12:30 AM. The only reason I did not have a hard time waking up, I think, is because I never got to sleep!

Eran led the charge, followed by Jeshua, Micaiah, and Jamin. They all plopped on our bed with, "GET UP! ITS CHRISTMAS!" A few minutes later we found Keithen, a 20 year old college sophomore sophisticate at the time, standing by the Christmas tree smiling broadly.

We had an exciting Christmas celebration. Our Christmas devotion and prayer came first. We gathered around the phone and called our oldest son, Ron, and daughter-in-law, Holly, about 4 AM, shouting simultaneously as they answered, "GET UP! ITS CHRISTMAS! We opened gifts, and had breakfast at 7 AM.

But, 2:54 AM stuck in my mind days following for a particular reason. On the grand scheme of things, 2:54 AM is not altogether significant since there were probably children in other homes attempting to roust parents at an even earlier time.

The point, however, is that our boys charged the steps earlier than Terry and I had expected. You may ask why we did not send them back to bed. That question I will answer momentarily.

Nonetheless, our family experience on Christmas morning 2000 brought to bear on an exciting spiritual truth from God's Word.

Jesus said, "Watch, therefore; for ye know not what hour your Lord doth come. Be ye ready; for in such an hour as ye think not the Son of man cometh."

For the believer in Jesus Christ, one of the logical considerations of the First Advent is the imminence of the Second Advent. In other words, the birth of Christ presupposes the Second Coming of Christ. In His first coming, Jesus was born in Bethlehem, divinity incarnated into human flesh for the purpose of redeeming man from sin. In His Second Coming, Christ is coming as King to rule and reign.

His first coming was dated, but His Second Coming is undated.

At what time will Jesus Christ come the second time? Will it be 2:54 AM? Will His Second Coming occur on a Monday? Will it be tomorrow? Next year, perhaps?

Are you even concerned about it?

I once discussed the Second Coming of Christ with a certain church attendee, who stated, "Don't get me wrong—I certainly believe that Jesus is coming back. I just hope He doesn't come back too soon. I have some more living to do."

This kind of attitude is certainly typical of those who are focused on the temporal rather than the eternal. The church-going breed of our day exemplifies a grave lack of concern for the things of God.

However, anticipation for the coming of Christ is a Christian requisite. As a matter of fact, the Crown of Righteousness will be rewarded at judgment to those that love His appearing. "But, ye, brethren, are not in darkness that that day should overtake you as a thief," said Apostle Paul.

I fully expect Jesus Christ to come again at any moment. I fully expect Jesus Christ to come again during my lifetime. Jesus said to Apostle John, "Surely, I come quickly." John replied, "Amen. Even so, come, Lord Jesus."

If the time of Christ's coming was near for the New Testament apostles and saints, how much closer are we to it with each passing year? I agree with John wholeheartedly.

Though Terry and I did not know that 2:54 AM would be the wake up time for this Christmas day, we fully expected an early call from the boys. In much the same way, though Christ's coming will be quick with the time unspecified, we should fully expect it. It will no doubt be an overwhelming joy for Christians when Christ comes again. He is not coming the second time to bear sin like He did the first time, but to bring salvation to fulfillment. I like and appreciate His intent!

Anyway, why did we not send the boys back to bed at 2:54 AM? It is because Terry and I were happy for the boys to come! We were prepared to get up with them. We had good things in store for them, and we were ready to share it with them.

By contrast, the blessed hope of the Second Coming of Christ is that He has worked and prepared good things for us. I believe He is excited about sharing them with us, and that makes me want to be ready to get up when He comes.

6

GOD CONFRONTS OUR INADEQUATE SPIRITUAL PERSPECTIVES

o o o o o o o o o o o o o o o o o o o o o o o o o o o o o o o o

"THE LORD GOD CALLED UNTO ADAM, AND SAID UNTO HIM, WHERE ART THOU?"

—(GENESIS 3:9)

IF I GET WORMS, I'M GOING TO BLAME YOU!

We once had a cat we kept in the garage at night. Each of the boys had the responsibility to alternately take care of the litter box before they went to school.

But, as matters usually transpire, we had to ride herd on them about it. They want pets, but the condition is that they take care of them, especially when it comes to this litter box upkeep.

One morning, Micaiah got up grumpy, and grumped through his pre-school preparations. When Terry reminded him about his cat chore turn, he demurred with obvious disdain. But, the firm threat of additional gleaning days convinced him to hesitate no longer.

Terry and I were sitting around the table waiting to have family devotions with the boys when he returned to the kitchen in a deeper state of grump. His mother reminded him to go and wash his hands. Though he did not want to bother with it, she insisted.

Before we realizied it, Micaiah was in the process of washing his hands in the kitchen sink over a clean pot Terry had earlier washed. She expressed her chagrin, and chided Micaiah that now she would have to rewash it. Again, he was told to go and wash his hands.

So, what did the boy do? He merely directed the faucet to the other sink, which contained breakfast dishes in soak, and continued the washing of his hands in the soapy water.

Upon seeing that, Terry blurted out, "Micaiah, I do say! Don't wash your hands there. If I get worms, I'm going to blame you!"

As Micaiah went finally to the bathroom to wash his hands, the combination of the situation in relation to the implication of what my good wife said struck me as funny. I burst out in laughter, nearly spilling hot coffee on my tie.

She walked to the sink and started draining the dishwater. "What's so funny?" she asked in an annoyed tone.

"Honey, that is a classic parental response to a child's misdoing if I have ever heard one," I replied teasingly.

Yet, as I thought on it, her statement rather captivated my attention. Where have I heard similar responses?

There is one in which a certain man claimed, "Lord, it is the fault of this woman you gave to be with me!" The man's name was Adam.

Another classic response comes from one, who essentially said, "Don't blame me. These people gave me their earrings, which I threw into the fire, and, lo and behold, out came this golden calf!" This gentleman had a famous brother named Moses.

Where the water meets the wheel concerns the tendency seemingly innate with us to direct blame to others for the shoddy circumstances in which we allow ourselves to become embroiled. As we have noted from Scriptural accounts, there have been some classic responses.

But, the similarities to our contemporary setting are quite obvious. Faced with the guilt of personal sin and its terrifying consequence, Adam is clearly typical of those who find it convenient to blame others for "ruining their lives."

Aaron, who glutted the fire with gold and, by his account, inadvertently produced a fat idol, is no different from those who gulp down an inordinate number of Big Macs and fries, and blame McDonalds for the obesity that comes out.

God does not tolerate one's willingness to blame others. "Every man shall bear his own burden," which serves as a reminder that we must assume full responsibility and give account for our own actions.

Terry fired back as she refilled the sink with sudsy water, "Well, Mr. Smartypants, why don't you do these dishes then?"

Unfortunately, because of my parents, who made me wash the dishes too many times when I was a kid, doing dishes is no longer something I can do. Would you believe it made my hands too sensitive?

<u>YOU WILL BE JUDGED!</u>

On Sunday mornings, I am very diligent to leave church-going preparations of the Branch boys to their lovely mother. There is a very good, ministerial reason for my early departure for church. I simply want to be in a Godly and spiritual frame of mind and heart when I get to church!

Many of you know what it is like to get kids ready for church on Sunday morning. You have to blast them out of bed. You have to hustle them to the breakfast table. Next there is the hassle over the bathroom. And, more often than not, parents invariably become embroiled with the children concerning their church attire.

Apparently, such happened with Terry and our son, Micaiah.

Micaiah used to be content in nothing less than dressing in his "handsome clothes" for Sunday services. He enjoyed wearing a little suit, shirt, and tie. But, he abandoned that mind-set, and began opting too often for too casual a clothing combo for church. Unfortunately, this became a point of stress between Mother and child. Terry had to apply a more hands-on oversight concerning it, particularly one Sunday morning when he was seven years old.

"Micaiah, I want you to get dressed in the church clothes I laid out for you. We will be leaving shortly," said Terry tersely.

Micaiah shuffled off to his room with another clothing agenda in mind, and roused up his most dilapidated pair of jeans, and a worn-out T-shirt. He had no problem with shoes, however, because he put on his best pair. Apparently content with his choice, he went upstairs headed to Jeshua's room.

When Terry passed him in the hallway, Terry was very discontented with his choice of clothes. Chagrined, she directed him back to his room to put on the designated attire.

Micaiah is prone to be argumentative at times, and, when he vocalized his disagreement, Terry gave a strong-worded, authoritative exhortation that he had better watch himself.

The second chance did not bring much change. Sitting on the edge of his bed, he re-verbalized his opinion about his attire.

Terry had had enough, and down the steps she charged. Micaiah backed under the cover of his bunk bed with trepidation. Terry stooped in toward him as he hunkered against the wall.

"Micaiah, I'm going to spank you!"

In that moment, it was as though Micaiah concluded that salvation from wrath to come required a standard Biblical backup. So, he cried out with the first Bible-based fact that raced into his mind, "IF YOU DO, THE BIBLE SAYS THAT **YOU WILL BE JUDGED!"**

Sometimes, disciplinary scenes with children become humorous. Forcing back laughter, Terry replied, "But, Micaiah, the Bible also says that a mother should 'Withhold not correction from the child: for if thou beat him with the rod, he shall not die.'"

So, what Scriptural truth is it that emerges from this Sunday morning, Branch-household incident?

It is found right in Micaiah's assertion to Terry, "**YOU** will be judged!" Although breaching his mother's instructions and stretching his mother's patience, he insisted that she would be the one judged.

Ironically, this is a typical, spiritual misperception. Too many are more apt to allege "you will be judged" rather than remembering "I will be judged!" While many are willing to breach the commands of God, they also are willing to assume a false consolation that others will be judged and not themselves.

But, the biting Bible truth is that every one of us will have to give a personal account before Jesus Christ.

II Corinthians 5:10 is one Biblical statement that affirms it, "For we must all appear before the judgment seat of Christ; that every one may receive the things done in his body, according to that he hath done, whether it be good or bad."

It prevails upon us to remember "I will be judged." There is something uncanny in spiritual effect when we truly understand what is eternally ahead of each of us. It not only minimizes arrogant attitude toward others, but also spurs us to set things right with God while striving to more diligently live out His assigned principles.

The prophet Amos is very direct on this point as he proclaimed, "Prepare to meet thy God" (Amos 4:12).

There is a solitary sidebar to the Mother/Micaiah meeting of minds.

Our son, Keithen, found the incident to be so funny that he told a friend at church what had happened.

Their observation was, "I would not want to get into an argument at your house, because, it would turn into a Scriptural debate, and I'd probably lose!"

WHAT IN THE WORLD ARE YOU THINKING?

One reason it is so much fun to watch kids play sports is because you never know exactly what they are thinking as the game unfolds before them.

Our son, Micaiah, who can run fast, played one season on a youth football team in the Big Bend Area league. His team did not begin well, but finished well.

Near season's end, his team played the league's top team. With five seconds left, the score was 0-0. On fourth down with about twenty yards to go for a touchdown, Micaiah remained in the backfield to block for his quarterback, who attempted a pass.

Unfortunately, it was intercepted, and, with no time on the clock, the defender started a mad dash for his goal line. He had a good angle for the side-line, and attained a lead ahead of blockers and tacklers. Parents and coaches for both sides were going nuts!

In the meantime, Micaiah just stood there and watched. I was both appalled and speechless that my boy was not in pursuit.

After the game, Terry asked him, "Micaiah, what in the world were you thinking out there," which is the same question posed all season by coaches to their players when multitudinous errors were made.

Micaiah replied that, looking up after having finished blocking, he thought it was his own teammate running with the ball.

That answer just did not jibe. There was a player with the other team's jersey running with the ball in the opposite direction. Players from his own team were running after and trying to tackle the boy with the ball. I grabbed my jaw and blinked my eyes hard to keep from saying something critical.

But, before any of us respond to Micaiah's on-field reasoning, we need to remember how our own spiritual reasoning must, in fact, cause the Lord to ask, "What are you thinking down there?"

God's people often do some incredibly dumb things in the arena of life that absolutely do not make any sense. If there is such a thing as spiritual brain-deadness, then we often show the symptoms of it.

This sad fact is exemplified in God's Word, as in the case of King Saul. Once, Saul erroneously took upon himself the role of priest to make an offering to the Lord before an important battle. In confronting Saul, Samuel asked, "What hast thou done?" In other words, "What in the world were you thinking about?" Saul had a simple-minded response when he said, "I forced myself."

Another time, Saul erred grievously when he absolutely failed to comply completely with God's war time instructions. What in the world was he thinking to defy God? Samuel said, "Listen, son, rebellion is as the sin of witchcraft, and stubbornness is as iniquity and idolatry."

Undoubtedly, life poses us with circumstances that involve choices. Sometimes, situations carry degrees of confusion and uncertainty. You find yourself tackling one issue, only to look up and find yourself confronted with having to chase after another.

Yet, the choices we make carry consequences.

However, such are the times we need to be patient and pray. Such are the times we need to stop long enough to consider the principles of God's Word. Such are the times we need to first prioritize the Lordship of Jesus Christ and the leadership of the Holy Spirit. Such are the times we need to make sure that what we are thinking coincides with what God is thinking.

It would save ourselves grief if we would, because, "The Lord is faithful, who shall stablish you, and keep you from evil."

Nonetheless, we left Micaiah standing and watching his opponent running toward the goal line for the winning touchdown. It finally occurred to him what was happening.

Suddenly, he took off running. He sped through his pursuing teammates and passed the blockers. After sprinting nearly forty yards, Micaiah caught up and made the tackle at the fifteen-yard line.

With a chuckle, Micaiah also told his mother, "But, I knew I could catch him!"

TEE TIME IS NOT THE TIME FOR A TIME OUT!

One of the distinct privileges I have is serving as chaplain for the Wahama High School football team, and then being able to stand along the sidelines during the games.

The only concern for the 2003 season was that two of my sideline cohorts were sons Micaiah and Jamin, who filled various chores in the team trainer tradition.

I was sure to make it abundantly clear to both of them that the work they did was important to the team. Therefore, they had to do their work well.

But, if they were going to work the sidelines, they also needed to be mindful of me. I did not want to be distracted needlessly from play on the field because of carelessness and frivolity on their parts. They were very aware that, if necessary, I will banish them to the upper regions of the home-side stands to sit with their Momma—an area I rarely venture myself!

Part of Micaiah's game responsibility was to take care of the tees. He was supposed to get the tees to the kickers for kickoffs and point-after attempts. It rather required that he pay attention to the game so that the kicks were able to transpire according to time standards.

During the second quarter of one Friday's game, Wahama scored a touchdown, and the point-after team lined up for the kick.

Suddenly, I noticed several of the players looking toward the sideline and gesturing with shrugged shoulders. Despite the din of fan celebration and band music, the question from the kicker wafted to the sidelines, "WHERE'S THE TEE?"

The next question was shouted by coaches and players alike up and down the line, "Where's Micaiah?"

Incredibly, Micaiah was standing down at the goal line where our team had scored. But, he was clearly not mindful of the situation because he was talking and laughing with a friend. As soon as he saw me heading toward him, he knew the mistake he had made, and started to run the tee out to the kicker.

But, it was too late. Wahama had to take a time out because the play clock was running down.

I sternly reprimanded Micaiah for not fulfilling his responsibility. But, then I put my arms around him, and said, "Son, you need to understand that a situation like this could have meant the difference between victory and defeat. If the score was close, and we did not have any more time outs, a critical opportunity could be missed for the team. You are too young to have to bear up under such an error. Do your job well!"

This incident possesses critical insight upon reflection.

One question often posed these days around religious circles is, "What is wrong with the church?" When it comes to spiritual, moral, and social issues, the church seems to have very little kick.

The problem is that too many of us among the church ranks are standing along the sidelines of the world with the tees of spiritual responsibility in our hands, not paying the necessary attention to the scoring opportunities about which the church should be taking advantage.

In so many terms, the church is charged by God to engage itself actively in the spiritual contest that is most certainly at hand. When Christ declared that "the gates of hell shall not prevail against it," the church was given the authority to be in the mode of vigorous attack against all that is contrary to God's will.

But, the needed interest is not there. To the Laodicean church, Christ termed it, "Thou art lukewarm."

The redeemed need to better fulfill spiritual responsibility. Do your work well. It is tee time! It is not time to have to take time for a time out.

THE DEVIL IS GOOD AT PUTTING STUFF IN FRONT OF OUR KIDS!

There have been instances in which one of our younger sons has noticed in a local convenience store a gambling machine that has several revolving shelves of quarters. A person gambles a quarter to see if "luck" will pay off in which a shelf will unload its holding of quarters.

Once, when he asked for a quarter from me for it, I told him that it was gambling, which was something he should never practice. God is too providentially gracious to our family to take what he gives us to gamble on the providence of man. When one considers the goodness of God, it is not only wrong, but it is not worth taking a chance on the gaming devices men construe for easy gain.

But, the devil can be providential, too, in the sneakiest of ways, and for the most vile of results.

Once, our youngster accompanied his oldest brother on an errand to this particular mart. On the way out, the boy found a quarter on the asphalt. Suddenly, he dashed back inside, and inserted the quarter in this gambling machine.

As "luck" would have it, he won $6.25. The incident appalled me. I do not want my boy getting caught up in a vice that has the future potential of developing into a harmful habit on the basis of gambling "luck" getting stuck in his young psyche.

However, this is but a small example of how good the devil is at putting stuff in front of my kids, like the coin and a chance for a case of quarters, and it makes me angry. But, he not only does this to my children, but to your children, too.

How is it that we parents can hope to deal with the devil's attempt to influence our children with evil?

Primarily, we parents must be good at putting the right kind of stuff in front our kids to countermand what the devil puts in front of our kids. One of the best ways to put the right kind of stuff in front of our kids is by way of teaching.

First, we parents must put in front of our children teaching that emphasizes making choices that are right and good. Times will be, when we are not present with them, that they will be confronted with decisions concerning evil influences. Our children need to know that when away from our immediate guidance we expect them to make the right choices.

Second, we parents must put in front of our children teaching that the right choices are always supported in the outlined principles and morals of the Bible. God's Word provides a guideline for blessed living, and many examples of those who were blessed because of the decisions they made on the basis of God's Word. The absolute truths of God always provide the best guidance for decision making.

Third, we parents must put in front of our children teaching that is diligent. That means we must teach and re-teach, say it and repeat it, go over it again and again. Why? Because, critical truths are generally not assimilated in a single session. The Scripture emphasizes this point. Concerning the commandments, God says, "And thou shalt teach them diligently unto thy children."

Fourth, we parents must put in front of our children teaching that is exemplified by our own example. It prevails upon us parents to be consistent models for our children. "Don't do as I do—do as I say" is one of the worst maxims for a parent to spout to children. Many of the ills that assail our society are the result of inconsistencies the next generation has seen from the previous generation.

That is why God is so great. Each generation has the privilege of seeing God as He has always been, and will always be. "I change not," God says. With God, there is no variableness, neither shadow of turning." We parents need to be more diligent in emulating God.

Undoubtedly, the devil is good at what he does. By God's grace, I will strive to do it better—for my children's sake. What about you?

<u>DON'T TELL THE BIRDS TO SHUT-UP!</u>

One of the ethical home practices my parents insisted was that we brothers were to not tell each other to "shut-up."

Terry and I have attempted to instill the same consideration in our boys, but they nonetheless inflict the verbal slam on each other all too often.

One morning recently, as we all were in the process of starting our day, I heard Micaiah from his bedroom blurt out, "Shut-up!"

I let it slide by without any response, and continued putting on my tie. But, it was not long before I heard Micaiah say again, "Shut-up!"

I gritted my teeth. I just did not feel like having to serve as referee so early in the day. Where was their mother?

I could only imagine that Jeshua was bossing Micaiah around about something, or that Jamin was humming one of his little tunes just to be an irritant. These boys of ours are constantly doing deliberate things to turn each other's screw.

Finally, Micaiah let it rip, "I said—SHUT-UP!

"What's going on in there?" I roared in response. That got the parental dander activated. I stomped across the hallway, and positioned myself in the doorway ready for action.

There sat Micaiah on the edge of his bed, with one leg crossed, putting on a sock. The window by his bed was open, and a cool breeze was blowing through the room. But, there was no one else in the room with him.

"Who are you telling to shut-up, son?" I asked sternly.

"I'm telling those stupid birds to shut-up. They are making me mad!" he replied.

Sure enough, birds could be distinctly heard cheeping and chirping outside, and having a big time tweeting about the start of their own day.

For a moment, I did not know what to say. The best I could come up with was, "Don't tell the birds to shut-up, because the happy sounds of birds are a blessing from God." Then, tongue-in-cheek, I added, "Besides, in Psalms it says that the birds "sing among the branches." Micaiah stared blankly at me.

While I can identify with Micaiah about having the grumps some mornings, his disposition toward the birds typifies the complaining attitudes people often have concerning the blessings of God.

For example, rain is a blessing, but we complain when the rain makes mud. The sun is a blessing, but we repine when its shine makes the temperature too hot. Life is a blessing, but we lament with discontent when all of it is not always convenient.

We need to be careful how we complain about the blessings of God. Scripture is instructive on this point as it recorded Israel's complaint about the Manna God supplied for their daily food during the years of their exodus.

So, God sent them birds, lots and lots of birds. God mustered up a great wind that blew in scads of quail for them to eat. But, the people soon lost their appetite, and the complaints started all over again.

This entire matter may be considered from the standpoint of Manna versus meat, or sunshine versus rain. But the question will always confront us—what would life be like without the simple, yet important, blessings of God?

Evelyn Roberts was a lady whose life experience involved one difficulty after another. After I became her pastor, she made a remarkable comment I have never forgotten.

She said, "Preacher, you might think I'm crazy, but, after I received Christ as my personal Lord and Savior, the next morning, for the first time in my life, I heard birds singing!"

Considering the alternatives, we need to be careful to never tell the birds to shut up.

7

GOD'S TRUTHS ARE NOT PARALIZING

o o o o o o o o o o o o o o o o o o o o o o o o o o o o o o o o o o o o

"THE TRUTH SHALL MAKE YOU FREE"

—(JOHN 8:32)

DISCOVER THE DIAMONDS IN THE DUNG!

Titus the bulldog belongs to our son, Ron, and daughter-in-law, Holly. Titus is a very expensive, English bulldog, and, despite his purebred qualities and papers, is just about as ugly as a dog can get.

Titus' ugliness, however, is super-ceded by his annoyance. One has to be constantly vigilant in his presence, because drool collects and hangs from the sides of his floppy mouth, and, periodically, when he shakes his head vigorously, he flings spittle everywhere and on everybody and on everything.

Ron is the only one who likes the dog. But, as things stand now, Holly is about ready to hang the dog.

One day, Holly realized she could not find her diamond engagement ring. She and Ron searched thoroughly their house, but without finding it.

Days later, one of Holly's necklaces came up missing, too. It was then that they started to suspect that Titus must have goat blood mixed in his specialized lineage, or, at the least, that Titus' tastes had taken on an expensive quality.

Nonetheless, Ron borrowed a metal detector, and began the pinging process in Titus' known pooping area. It amuses me to envision my son scanning canine dung for diamonds, but it was not long before the detector identified a certain hardened glob that surprisingly yielded a dime.

In short time, Ron retrieved two more dimes and a nickel, which Titus had ingested and eventually discharged. It was not long before he pulled the necklace out of another doggy pile, and, right before he was about to quit the search, he disengaged Holly's diamond engagement ring from another drop site.

With tongue-in-cheek, it is easy to surmise that good has come out of a messy situation. But, it certainly goes beyond such a trite conclusion since it provides the means, with Scripture's perspective, to remind us that God works beneficently in our own lives. When we trust God, we, too, are given the means whereby we may discover diamonds in the dung. Why is this true?

Many of us know well how sometimes it appears as though the prospects and hopes of life are consumed by unsettling circumstances. At times, difficulties consume us as a result of no apparent reason. At other times, the decisions we make ourselves result in undesirable consequences.

Yet, such are the times we want to complain that our life's valuable time and possibilities have taken on a dung-like quality. "Life stinks!" some say. "If life is supposed to be so good, why am I standing knee-deep in you-know-what?" we pine. In so many terms, we want to blame God for letting our lives become ravaged and expelled like so much excrement.

Regardless, we have a profound choice. We can settle for the poop we perceive to be encasing our lives, or we can opt to trust God to discover the diamonds in the dung.

Romans 8:28 states, "And we know that all things work together for the good of them that love God." Not all things are good, but in all things God works to bring out good in our lives. It is something God never fails to deliver to people of faith.

From Scripture's stories, I'm sure that Mary Magdalene, whose life was once consumed with so much evil, could tell you about the beautiful diamonds she discovered as a consequence of trusting the Lord. The same would be true of the Maniac of Gadara, who received eternal life in a graveyard. Even the Prodigal Son stepped out the pig poop to have a ring of restored fellowship placed on his finger.

Indeed, if you want to look at your life as some sort of manure site, so be it. But, if you give God a chance, He will provide you some exciting discoveries.

As far as Titus is concerned, however, he remains a pain in the butt!

WE ARE TOO EASILY DUMBFOUNDED!

Titus is the pure bred English bulldog that belongs to our eldest son, Ron. None of us in the family can understand why Ron likes the dog so well. Titus requires an inordinate amount of care, is a gross irritant to be around, and is absolutely dumb as dirt. Sometimes Ron has to admit it is true.

For instance, after one has bathed, Titus likes to jump into the shower and lick up the water. This makes Ron mad, and prompts him to fuss at his dog. Titus is very sensitive to when Ron's fusses at him, but the dog never seems to learn that shower water-licking is prohibited.

Once, Ron took a late night shower after a long day, and, true to form, Titus plopped in the tub right after Ron got out. Ron was so weary, he just, in a fit of disgust with Titus, pulled the shower curtain across the rod, and went to bed.

Ron was up early the next morning and out of the house for a few hours. When he returned, he could not find Titus. He looked in the places Titus likes to sleep. He checked out the basement. He took a brief look around the yard for his pet.

When he could not find Titus, it occurred to him to check out the shower. Sure enough, when he pulled back the shower curtain, there sat Titus looking up at him. Ron surmises that Titus thought a door had been shut on him, and could not get out.

Now, to you dog lovers, this might seem like a cute thing. But, to me, the fact that Titus was dumbfounded by no more than a shower curtain for almost 15 hours, believing he could not get out of his predicament, proves dirt dumbness.

Evidently, Titus did not even try. He never barked. He merely sat there and moped—ugly face, slobbering jaws, and all.

Sad to say, however, we are very much the same way many times. We are too easily dumbfounded by hindrances that are merely shower-curtain strong, and all we do is mope, moan, and mumble about malady and misfortune.

God's Word gives us a great example from the experience of Israel at Kadesh-Barnea the first time they approached the Promised Land.

You know the story. Twelve spies were commissioned to check out the territory. They brought back a glowing report. The land was great! But, they would never be able to take the land as God commanded because of the giants that lived there, according to the intimidating report of ten scouts.

They were immediately dumbfounded! "There we saw the giants, and we were in our own sight as grasshoppers, and we were in their sight."

Size became the shower curtain drawn across their path to all that God had promised. The giants and their own grasshopper perspective dumbfounded them. Consequently, they wound up being a horde of dumbfounded people sitting in the wilderness for thirty-eight years, before the curtain was finally pulled back to where they could see how easy it was to get out of their predicament. Ultimately, they found that the size of the giants proved no barrier at all.

How easily dumbfounded are you? What specifically dumbfounds you like some sort of flimsy shower curtain? Financial concerns? Family problems? Lack of self-esteem?

If we are ever going to be the fruitful and victorious people God has in mind for us, we continually must muster gutsy spiritual fortitude such that reaches up to swipe back the hindrance, and the sooner set us free. With God, you can do something about it right now!

Otherwise, we will remain dumbfounded on our haunches like ol' Titus—ugly face, slobbering jaws, and all—just licking up shower water.

THAT'S A SQUIRREL OF A DIFFERENT FEATHER!

Hunting is a great privilege. It is also a relaxing pastime—unless you are a man who has to take noisy children out in the attempt to demonstrate what is involved with successful hunting. Sons Micaiah and Jamin once proved particularly difficult to teach the value of stealth in the hunting process.

For example, the first thing both would do as they entered the woods was to retrieve for themselves a sturdy stick. With these sticks, they karate-whacked every tree they passed, just like the Power Rangers did to those mutant miscreants on afternoon, after school TV.

These two also added the vocals, along with leaf-throwing and rock bombing. These boys wanted me to take them hunting so they could watch their Dad bag a squirrel. Go figure.

One day, when I was with them on the hill behind the house, I came to a stop to take a token look around. I happened to notice a hawk feather lying on the ground close by.

It was then that Micaiah decided to raise a word of complaint.

"Dad, we're not seeing any squirrels! How come?" he asked sharply.

About that time, Jamin started hollering, "Micaiah! Micaiah! I know for sure there are squirrels around here. Look at this—I HAVE FOUND A SQUIRREL FEATHER!"

I lost it with laughter at that point.

"Put that thing down, Jamin," Micaiah responded, "That's not a squirrel feather. That's a bird feather! There's no such thing as a squirrel feather."

"It is, too!" Jamin said as he bellied up to Micaiah defiantly.

So, while we were supposed to be squirrel hunting, they got into a brief bickering spree. The one was sure that squirrels were around because he had a squirrel feather to prove it, and the other maintained that, while squirrels were around, squirrels did not have feathers.

Finally, Jamin looked up at me, and asked, "Dad, this is a squirrel feather, isn't it?"

You know, I could have gone along with Jamin, and told him that it was indeed a squirrel feather. But, it would have only bred continued confusion for both boys.

"No, son, it isn't. It is a hawk feather. Squirrels don't have feathers."

Jamin let the feather drop to the ground, and we resumed our hunt.

Once we were home I told Terry about what Jamin had said. It was then that she quipped, "That was a squirrel of a different feather!"

While I have no idea where Jamin came up with this belief about squirrel feathers, it nonetheless confronts us all with a grave spiritual concern, for there are a good many these days who are coming up with squirrels of a different feather, too.

It is very clear that our nation is embroiled in moral controversy and confusion. It seems as though we have little concept of right and wrong, as well as difficulty in discerning what truth is.

While we are suppose to be on a hunt in life for what is best for society, it seems that society is full of squirrel feathers.

Consider the following squirrel feathers being found today.

"The gambling industry creates needed jobs!" Yet, gambling is addictive.

"Pornography is a matter of free speech and artistic expression!" Yet, pornography is destructive to homes and personalities.

"God is not needed in our educational system!" Yet, problems in our schools worsen.

"The legalization of civil unions is not the same as same sex marriages!" Yet, the God-ordained ideal of marriage and home are being undermined.

"A fetus is not a human being!" Yet, the tension in the national conscience is not assuaged.

Such political, economic, and moral positions are squirrels of a different feather. Those who argue they have a squirrel feather in hand are those who are not stopping long enough to ask the Father, "Is this a squirrel feather or not?"

The sober concern is that our contemporary circumstances do not provoke humor. God is not amused. On every point or opinion that are not consistent with Godliness and righteousness, God states the truth, "That is not a squirrel feather!" It is God who tells the truth—if only we will listen. Most, apparently, are not willing to listen.

A couple of days later, when it was just Jamin and me hunting, he happened to see a squirrel before I did. When I teasingly asked him if the squirrel had feathers, he whacked me on the rear with the stick he had.

He will be reminded about squirrel feathers for a while!

WE FOUND ANOTHER SQUIRREL FEATHER!

Have you ever noticed how it seems so hard for people to learn point-specific lessons of life? Our son, Jamin, gave full proof to this observation nearly a year after he had found his "squirrel feather."

I thought that the boy had learned a fact about hunting game, but apparently it did not register with him well enough.

Nonetheless, it was another pleasant October afternoon as I walked with the three younger boys, Jeshua, Micaiah, and Jamin, to spend some time with them.

Jeshua carried his .22 rifle just in case a squirrel showed itself, and the other two had their BB guns to shoot at trees and chipmunks

Jamin was immediately behind me when I stopped and pointed to the ground at a hawk feather lying on top of the leaves.

Turning to him, I pointed, and said with a chuckle, "Look, Jamin. Here is another squirrel feather."

I thought for sure that he would fuss at me for teasing him.

But, instead, he turned around to Micaiah with excitement, and exclaimed loudly, "Micaiah, get ready! There has got to be a squirrel around here. Dad found another squirrel feather!"

I could not believe it. As Jeshua and I burst out in laughter, Micaiah sternly reminded his brother that squirrels did not have feathers.

"You ought to know that by now!" he said.

Now, one would automatically think he should have known better after being teased, corrected, and instructed all year about squirrel feathers.

Yet, his child-likeness is no worse than that of Christians who prove themselves to possess a similar simpleness.

You see, God has made it perfectly clear what His expectations are of the redeemed. We have been bought by the precious price of Christ's death on the Cross. The gift of eternal life and its pursuant blessings for now did not come cheaply. Because of Christ, God expects us to live according to His gracious and beneficent principles.

Another matter God has made perfectly clear is that, if we fail to live according to His plans and purposes for us, He will work in such ways so as to regain our spiritual attention and restore our sense of devotion. Chastening is the Biblical term.

Yet, when God deals with us, it is many times the case that we continue to live the same old way outside of God's will as though we never learned a thing.

One of the great failures, for example, of our contemporary Christian circumstances involves periodic unfaithfulness to God.

We have the mindset that we can live any way we choose, and, when troublesome times occur, all we have to do is utter the perceived magical cure-all prayer, "My God, we know thee" (Hosea 8:3).

But, God, through the prophet Hosea asserts, "My people are destroyed for a lack of knowledge…for they have forgotten the law of God."

"Knowledge," as it relates to God, refers to daily and intimate relationship with God, and typically involves faithfulness to that pursuit.

There are tremendous spiritual ramifications when we think we can opt to forget God for a season. Times are when we should learn from the lessons the Lord teaches us concerning it to ensure that we not repeat the same errors.

Mark it well—it makes a big difference to perceive crises as being the onslaughts of satanic afflictions rather than God's corrections. With the former, we stand in the victory of God. With the latter, we experience the rebuke of God.

Once the laughter subsided, we got back in row on the trail.

"Dad," Jamin asked, "Is there not such a thing as a flying squirrel?"

"Why, yes, there is," I replied.

"Well, I bet you that was a flying squirrel feather then!" he offered.

God help me. I will be 60 years old when the boy graduates high school—that is, if I make that long.

8

GOD GIVES GREAT BLESSING

○ ○

"HE SATISFIETH MY MOUTH WITH GOOD THINGS"

—(PSALMS 103:5)

HE WAS THANKFUL FOR WHAT WAS IN THE POT!

I can't cook worth a hoot beyond bacon and eggs, or oatmeal and grits. My boys know that for a fact right well. As a matter of fact, Keithen wrote a paper when he was in high school about how bad pancakes can be when I make them. That is why on occasion I have said that I cook best when we eat out! My wife, Terry, has come to expect I will lead the boys on a Kentucky Fried chicken tour when she is not at home.

Several years ago, Micaiah was grievously ill and in the hospital for nearly three weeks. While Terry ministered to him, I tended matters at home. It was one particular evening during that stretch that it occurred to me just how distasteful the meals I prepared were to the boys.

A lady by the name of Sandra Cokely dropped off a pot of creamed lima beans. The boys hit that pot of creamed lima beans like a blight! I couldn't get over it. How many kids do you know who will eat a bowl full of creamed lima beans without being threatened? In retrospect, I don't believe either of them has eaten a lima bean since.

Before our meals, we usually call on one to give God a thanksgiving for something during the day, and then one of us prays thanksgiving for the food before us.

Eran volunteered as we gathered around the counter, "Dad, let me give God a thanks."

"Alright, go ahead, Son."

"I thank the Lord for the creamed lima beans we got!" he said.

Next, Jeshua, who was five years-old at the time, was called on to pray. He prayed for a variety of things, especially for Micaiah and Mom.

But, then raising his little voice in a preachy sort of way, he prayed, "And, LO-O-RD! We are so-o-o thankful for what is in THIS pot. We give you thanks for the woman who thought enough of us boys to fix us this WONDERFUL pot of creamed lima beans! Help these lima beans to nourish our bodies. Thank you so much, LO-O-RD! Amen."

I think I got my feelings hurt a little bit. Apparently, my "creative leftovers casserole" did not look very appetizing to them.

But, I have to admit that those creamed lima beans sure hit the spot. I thanked the Lord for them, too. God knows how to refresh His people in unique ways.

After all these years, we reminisce at times about that time of crisis, and still give God thanks for that pot of creamed lima beans.

The Psalmist said, "It is a good thing to give thanks unto the Lord" (Psalms 92:1).

One of the factors which motivates me to spend a portion of my day in prayer is to have the formal opportunity to give God thanks for all that He does for my family and me. I am grateful for what God has put, puts, and will put in our pot, so to speak.

We give God thanks that Terry and I, all the boys, and our daughters-in-law, Holly and Jessica, have been saved by the precious sacrifice of Jesus Christ. We are grateful for the strength and supply He provides through every crisis we experience. He has shared beneficently His peace and love in our family. When we fuss amongst ourselves, His love in our midst keeps us tight. He has provided for us exceedingly abundantly above what we have asked or thought (Ephesians 3:20). We thank Him for our nation. We are especially grateful for health. Prospects for good in the future provide for us reasons to raise up words of thankfulness. The Branch family makes it a point to give God thanks for His providential care.

It is good ethically to give God thanks, because God deserves it. As Jesus pointed out that God takes care of the sparrow, how much more does He take care of us. People who are truly thankful understand that God is the source and supply of all that we have.

"I have been young, and now am old; yet have I not seen the righeous forsaken, nor his seed begging bread./He is ever merciful, and lendeth; and his seed is blessed" (Psalms 37:25-26).

It is good practically to give God thanks, because it helps us to maintain proper perspective. The Psalmist pointed out that God owns the cattle on a thousand hills. In dispersing His blessings on mankind, it is clear that some have come into more cattle than others. But, if we are truly thankful for our specific blessings, God somehow gives us the perspective that we are blessed above all others. We do not have to be jealous of what someone else has. Class envy is a non-issue. "A brutish man knoweth not; neither doth a fool understand this" (Psalms 92:6).

It is good emotionally to give God thanks, for it lifts the heart. This is particularly effective when it is remembered that thanksgiving is not necessarily given for what God has done, but specifically for what God is going to do. You may be concerned about how certain things are going to be taken care of. You may be unsure about the days ahead. But, expressions of thanks for what you expect God to do fills one with faith and encouragement. It is always uplifting to give thanks today for tomorrow.

"Bless the Lord, O my soul: and all that is within me, bless His holy name. Bless the Lord, O my soul, and FORGET NOT ALL HIS BENEFITS" (Psalms 103:1-2).

Once, when Keithen was home from college on Thanksgiving break, he filled a big pot with delicious cookies from the schools cafeteria. When he arrived home, the cookie pot was given over Jamin, who exclaimed, "You're the best brother in the whole wide world!" He was particularly thankful for what was in the pot.

Undoubtedly, when you look into your own pot of life, you can easily be thankful for what God has put there, and understand that He is the best God in all of the universe.

CONCERNING CASES OF CONVENIENCE

Consider this question: when is it most convenient to receive a hot pan of luscious lasagna and a long loaf of well-seasoned garlic bread?

It was April, 1994, and the Branch family had a particularly hard week. Each of us experienced maladies to various degrees. Terry had surgery. Jamin spent time in the hospital with a viral infection.

Consequently, home duties fell on Dad's shoulders in addition to the work of the ministry.

The Wednesday of that particular week was involved with a funeral, which took up considerable time and travel. Afterwards, I rushed home to prepare supper for the boys coming home from school. We needed to eat quickly in order to prepare for Wednesday evening church. I tried to calmly deal with the stress.

As I hurriedly attempted to evoke a meal from leftovers, it suddenly occurred to me that there was an unusual quietness. I did not hear Micaiah, two years old at the time, making any racket. I became suspicious.

"Eran!" I said. "Go see if you can find Micaiah!"

Eran found Micaiah in Keithen's room.

"He is in here, Dad. You better come."

A deep dread filled my emotion.

I calmly turned off the burners. Dad's famous concoction of leftover food materials had to hold a while.

It seemed to get real hot all of a sudden. So, I loosened my tie as I stepped across the living room to search out the boy.

Sure enough, there was Micaiah postured against the window. He was obviously regressing from previous instructions concerning proper potty-training procedures.

I picked him up very carefully, holding him out in front of me as I headed toward the bathroom for an unwanted cleaning chore. I successfully stymied brimming complaint at Micaiah.

Suddenly, the phone rang.

"It's for you, Dad!"

I moaned and groaned. What timing!

"Micaiah, you stand still. Don't you move! Eran, come and make sure Micaiah doesn't move."

I picked up the phone. It was a lady from our church, Robin Petty.

"You fixed lasagna and garlic bread for us? Man, that's great! You want to bring it now? Yes, indeed. Bring it on down. See you later." Oh, my, I had to hurry, because she lived very close to us.

Back to the bathroom I stepped to resume my heavy-handed chore. Micaiah had not moved, to my surprise.

But, the phone rang again.

"Dad, it is for you!"

"Son, get their name and number, and tell them I will call them back," I replied with soiled panties in one and toilet paper in the other.

"They can't, Dad. It is long distance." Thus, I yielded to the request.

I stepped to the phone with the toilet paper roll under one arm and the soiled panties between my fingers to avoid contaminating myself.

As I picked up the receiver, I remembered to moor Micaiah.

I turned and spoke sternly in the direction of the bathroom, "Son, you stay still now!" To enforce it, I once again dispatched Eran go make sure, to his clear chagrin.

Eran muttered something about it inconveniencing him, but I had to let it pass.

Then, Jeshua complained, "Dad, I'm hungry! When are we going to eat?"

My facial expression let him know that his question was most certainly poorly timed. I was feeling hard pressed to keep the stress in control.

The person on the phone was a church member calling from the Cleveland Clinic. He wanted me to hear the good news about his wife. I rejoiced with him. When someone has praise for God, it prevails upon one to participate in the praise. "Rejoice with those who rejoice," says the Scripture, which does not include any thought about a convenient timetable.

When I returned to the bathroom, I found that Micaiah had climbed back on the toilet to complete matters. It would have helped tremendously if he had started there in the first place.

Just as he was ready for me to restore him hygienically, there was a knock on the door. What timing, I thought as I rolled my eyes. It was Robin with the lasagna and bread. I asked her to set it on the counter since I was not in the proper hygienic condition myself to handle food—if you know what I mean!

Suddenly, Micaiah came streaking through the living room in a state of unhindered, fleshly glory. In one hand was a four-foot section of toilet paper, flying and flopping in the breeze stirred up by his run in and around the living room furniture. Feeling free and relieved, he squealed and chirped happily. He concluded his run by latching onto and hugging my leg. Totally embarrassed, I tried to shift him behind me as much as possible.

As Robin departed, I thanked her for her thoughtfulness in preparing a meal for us. Inwardly, I thanked God for His great grace, which helped me to endure with mind and emotion in tack.

Now, back to the question: when is it most convenient to receive a hot pan of luscious lasagna and long loaf of well-seasoned garlic bread?

The answer is obvious—anytime at all, regardless of the circumstances!

But, all of this was told because a question of greater importance prevails upon us. The question is, "When is it most convenient to respond to God?"

Is not convenience a concern to most people when it comes to responding to God?

Acts 24 records that Apostle Paul advocated the Gospel of Christ before Felix, the Roman procurator of Judea at the time. His trembling revealed obvious conviction about his need for Christ.

But, Felix ultimately responded by saying to Paul, "Go your way for this time. When I have a convenient season, I will call for you."

Such reveals a pervasive attitude with many people. It is not always convenient to respond to God. There is too much going on. There is too much busy-ness. Timing is not right. Headaches and heartaches are distracting. There are too many matters to occupy the mind.

Consider it from this standpoint. Would I not have been naïve to tell Robin that it was inconvenient for her bring that pan of lasagna and loaf of garlic bread? After all, I am a terrible cook, about which my boys will readily admit. Furthermore, the thought of leftovers was not very palatable to any of us. If I had told Robin to wait till next time, there may not have been a next time.

Consider, also, that, if I had refused to talk and rejoice with the caller because it was inconvenient for me, he may have never wanted to confide in his pastor ever again.

By contrast, people just do not know how foolish they are to tell a caring and loving God that it is just not a very convenient time for salvation, for rededication, or any other spiritual matter about which He may speak to us.

The Scripture warns, "You seek the Lord while He may be found. You call upon Him while He is near."

You see, salvation is a matter which deserves immediate response. God through Christ prepared a great salvation for our benefit. Deliberate delays to more convenient times are very foolish. A person could possibly die before that convenient time arrives. God's Spirit could possibly cease striving with a person before that convenient time comes.

Godly blessings deserve immediate response. Many times powerful blessings are missed because it is not convenient to fully trust God. Many times God desires to bless us when it is very inconvenient, such as times of upsets, disappointments, and trials.

Come to think about it, my boys and I may not have ever known just how great a lasagna Robin makes if Jamin had not become ill.

I certainly do not desire ill health for my family. But, clearly, the lasagna represents a caring and loving blessing from the Lord through Robin when our family was undergoing a very tense time.

So, when should it be most convenient to respond to God?

Right now!

When God deals with you, respond right now. Do not wait for a more convenient season—for it may never arrive.

Do not be like Felix.

Remember the saga of Robin's lasagna.

YOU WANT TO PAY ME?

Jamin, four-year old at the time, had been good as gold. He had been playing by himself for nearly an hour. He hummed and sang while he played. As a parent, I found it rather inspiring.

Isn't that what you want your children to do when they are in the house? You want them to be good while they play without the fussing and fighting and generally jarring the house to pieces. Right? A parent expects that their children be good. Right?

Apparently, the same thing occurred to Terry. I heard her walk by and compliment him, "Jamin, you have been such a good little boy the last little while!"

Without compulsion, Jamin replied, "I know! You want to pay me?"

Though Terry and I simultaneously burst forth in laughter, this little incident highlighted a spiritual imperative.

It is inherent in the mind-set of many Christians that righteous performances should be rewarded by God. In other words, if we are good in certain ways and for prescribed periods of time, then God should pay us.

We see such philosophy typified by the three "friends" who visited Job when that good man was afflicted by Satanic evil. From their humanistic perspective of life, a man became well-off because he was good. They tried to insist that Job's sufferings were the direct result of wicked behavior, and that God was afflicting him with retribution.

Nothing could be farther from the truth. Job recognized the truth by making two profound affirmations of faith. First, he said, "The Lord gave, and the Lord hath taken away; blessed be the name of the Lord" (1:21). Second, he said, "Though He slay me yet will I trust in Him" (13:15). Regardless of the circumstances, Job still expected to be good, to fear God, and to reject evil (1:1).

The people of God who practice good do not expect pay from God. People practicing the good of God are moral people who understand that God expects moral living, are spiritual people who understand that God expects spiritual living, and are Spirit-controlled people who understand that God expects Spirit-controlled living.

Proverbs 22:1 states that "A good name is rather to be chosen than great riches."

Yet, all too often, many who profess Christ ultimately turn from practicing good simply because of their perception that God has not done enough to honor what they perceive as their good efforts. In the spiritual scheme of it all, these show themselves to be mercenaries rather than true Christian soldiers.

The bottom line is that the Christian who practices the good of God builds for themselves riches in Heaven that cannot be measured by what a dollar is or how the stock market does.

As far as Jamin is concerned, however, I slipped him a quarter later on without explanation. I would not want to misrepresent principle to him.

But, one thing for sure, his being good was worth a million bucks to Terry and me. I suppose we two rather turned out to be the bandits of benefit on this deal.

9

GOD IS ALWAYS THE ANSWER TO ALL OUR QUESTIONS

o o o o o o o o o o o o o o o o o o o o o o o o o o o o o o o

"CANST THOU DRAW OUT LEVIATHAN WITH A HOOK? CANST THOU PUT A HOOK INTO HIS NOSE?"

—(JOB 41:1-2)

FINGERS AND STRAWS

"Dad, why do you plant these plants?" Micaiah questioned as helped me in the garden.

"If you don't plant them, they die," I responded.

"Yes, but how do they live in the dirt?"

A child often expects specific answers to complicated questions causing one to dig for simple explanations.

I was planting cauliflower, and I revealed the strands of roots that held the potting soil tight.

"These are roots. Roots are like fingers and straws. A plant digs its fingers into the dirt."

I demonstrated by running my fingers into the soil and flexing them. "They grab the dirt so the plant won't be blown away by the wind or moved by the rain.

"A plant's roots are also like straws sucking up food from the dirt." I continued by making a long slurping sound. "The foods in the dirt make it possible for the plant to produce food we can eat."

Micaiah extended his fingers in the loose soil and slurped, too.

And, in that moment, I sensed God's hand planting in the soil of my own spirit a vital spiritual truth. I recalled Isaiah 17:31, which says, "Take root downward, and bear fruit upward."

Just like Micaiah's concern about a young plant's growth in dirt, so are Christians often perplexed with the issue of spiritual growth in Christ.

A born-again believer is the result of the seed of the Gospel germinating regeneration. The vital outgrowth following one's salvation dictates that progressive growth in Christ occur, which concerns and confuses many.

Thus, through a child's level of understanding, we can compare growth in Christ to fingers and straws.

Like finger roots thrusting deeper in the soil of salvation, we anchor ourselves to the stability of Christ with a flex-firm grasp on His principles demonstrated in the Bible.

Like straws, we absorb spiritual nourishment from the unending blessings and spiritual nutrients of abundant life in Christ.

Like a plant attaining unity with the soil, so does a Christian attain a unity with Christ. How powerful Paul's words at this point, "We have been planted together in the likeness of His death" (Romans 6:5).

All the while, this fingers-and-straws experience becomes an important process: fruit-bearing!

Yes, I look forward to tomatoes and potatoes from my garden. I expect that each plant use their fingers and straws to produce fruit and vegetables.

And, no less expectation does Christ have of those Christians who have been planted in Him—"BEAR FRUIT UPWARD."

No circumstance hinders a Christian planted in Christ from bearing fruit.

Oh, yes, excessive winds may blow down my corn. Excessive rains may drench my melons. Excessive heat may wilt my lettuce.

But, when one considers life in Christ, the greater the adversity the greater the fruit produced in that believer who has spiritual fingers and straws woven and laced in Christ.

Fingers and straws made sense to a child eager to learn why plants grow.

May it suggest to us an urgency to understand what it means for us who are planted in Christ.

WHY HAS GOD MADE TICKS TO SUCK OUR BLOOD?

When Micaiah was four years old, Terry one day found a tick on him. It was then that she took the time to explain the importance of being alert to ticks, because ticks will bite and will cause serious illness to humans.

After a few minutes passed, Micaiah walked over to his mother, and looking up, he simply asked the question "Why?"

Terry responded, "Why about what, Micaiah?"

"Why do ticks bite people?" he wanted to know.

So, Terry explained that God made ticks to suck blood for survival.

The explanation apparently threw the youngster into the realm of unexplained theological questions, because, as he wondered out loud, "Why would God make a tick to suck my blood?"

Micaiah actually was somewhat offended at God.

It does make one wonder since ticks are usually unseen grass-and-weed critters that drop on you before you know it. Then, they look for the most vulnerable body point they can find just to fill their craws at our expense, sometimes leaving infection as a consequence of their thirst for blood.

However, though the issue was far from being satisfactorily explained to Micaiah on that particular summer afternoon about God's role and reason in making ticks, there is an important matter to consider in light of it.

It is found in the fact that Micaiah is still going to church. He is still singing about Jesus. He is still learning about the Bible. He is still making his child-like progress in faith in God.

An unanswered question about why God would make a tick to suck his blood has not hindered Micaiah and his budding relationship with God.

By contrast, it is the unfortunate result with many people that, when they come to have unanswered and unexplained questions, they essentially turn their backs on God. They refuse to have any more to do with Him.

In this day and age when scientific and technological explanations are given almost daily, it is as if it is now ingrained in the human expectations of life to have God explain Himself before we consider Him worthy enough to be embraced.

This is just in many respects a trick of the human trade, whereby people think they can control God with a question, and vindicate themselves from having to fulfill the spiritual responsibility most everyone senses we have before God.

Nonetheless, people often ask me some pointed God-related, Bible-related questions about which I do not have answers. Out of grief, sometimes out of bitterness, at other times because of disappointment, people feel that it is imperative to have explained to them why it appears as though God caused a tragedy or did not prevent heartache.

But, my question is, "Do we need to have everything explained in detail to us just so we may decide to have relationship with God and faith in God?"

I think that it is very interesting a question that God put to Job. God asked, "Does the rain have a father?" It is not only an interesting question, but also noteworthy that God did not give it a detailed explanation in order that Job would have deeper faith.

There are several facts that satisfy my soul as I, too, have to deal with the complexities of life. First, the evil events that occur are not God's fault. The blame belongs to Satan. Second, Jesus Christ died and rose again that I may possess the hope of eternal life. Third, I am convinced that God loves me. Fourth, God is absolute Sovereign.

Says the Scripture, "Touching the Almighty, we cannot find Him out. He is excellent in power, and in judgment, and in plenty of justice. He does not afflict."

These facts make unanswered questions unimportant.

CAN JESUS HIT A GOLF BALL 300 MILES?

We live across the road from the 4th tee of the Riverside Golf Course just outside Mason, WV. From our vantage on the hill, we often hear the cheers and fusses of the golfers, the whack of shots hitting trees, and the tinny whines of golf carts moving about the course. Sometimes an errant shot winds up in our yard.

I do not play golf well at all. The last time I played the Riverside course I gave up counting strokes on the 15th hole after I had reached something around 140! My presence on a golf course is usually the result of a gracious invitation by those who just happen to want to include me in their play for the day.

One day, I was with friends when we came to the 4th tee across from the house. Jamin, six years old at the time, was on the front porch playing, and we all called to him. He ran quickly to the front door to tell others in the house that he saw us. By the time it was my turn to tee up, the family was on the porch to watch.

As usual, my tee shot was a disaster. On my swing, I topped the ball, and hooked a scorching dribbler that went only about 40 yards, ripping through the weeds and bounding somewhere onto the railroad track. One of the men told me not to be discouraged, because I was assuredly getting better all the time.

I dropped another ball at an approximate location where my first shot went out of bounds. I really laid into the next stroke, but I sliced it at about a 65-degree angle onto the adjoining fairway. After that, we were out of the family's sight.

When I got home, Jamin was playing around with an old #3 iron. Dragging the club across the concrete, he walked up to me and asked a curious question, "Dad, can Jesus hit a golf ball 300 miles?"

His question almost caused me to choke with laughter, but I answered him seriously, "Yes, Jesus can hit a golf ball 300 miles if He wants to."

His question was not complete. "Well, can he steer it, too?"

"Yes, He can steer it if He wants to."

"I was just wondering," he said. Then, he went on playing his little game.

I stood there momentarily a little flabbergasted with his question. Why would he wonder about Jesus' golfing ability? Kids often come up with some doozy questions about God, Jesus, and spiritual and Scriptural concerns, which make you wonder what is going on in their minds.

But, we have questions, too, do we not? It is just, that as we get older, our spiritual questions take on a serious tone, which reflects our innate concern for relating properly to God. Furthermore, there are those questions we have which, if we had an answer, facilitate a sense of comfort and connection with God here and now.

For example, a question often asked is, "Is Heaven a real place?" That is an understandable question, because Heaven is not like a demonstration home you can walk through and examine today. Personally, I have never seen Heaven with my eyes, I have not walked on the street in Heaven, nor have I felt anything in Heaven with my hands

However, based upon the authority of God's Word, there is an answer to the question, because Heaven is a real place undeniably verified.

The Apostle Paul testifies He saw Heaven (II Corinthians 12:1-4). The Apostle John saw Heaven, too, in such detail so as to give the prospect of Heaven a rather exciting and glowing description.

We read about it in Revelation 21 and 22. John's description reveals that Heaven is not only a large place, but also an unparalleled facility with an unparalleled quality of life, and inhabited with a people of unparalleled quality of character.

Heaven, wrote John, is a lavish city with jeweled walls, jeweled foundations, jeweled gates, and a golden street. Heaven is a place of light, a place of life, a place of freedom, a place of worship, and a place of service.

But, above everything else, Heaven is where Jesus is, and the people there "see His face" (Revelation 22:4).

Is Heaven a real place? Recall the words of Jesus Himself, who said, "Let not your hearts be troubled: ye believe in God, believe also in me./In my Father's house are many mansions: **IF IT WERE NOT SO, I WOULD HAVE TOLD YOU**. I go to prepare a place for you./And, if I go and prepare a place for you, I will come and receive you unto myself; **THAT WHERE I AM YE MAY BE ALSO**" (John 14:1-3).

The reality of Heaven is a blessed hope given to us by Jesus Christ. Biblical hope is not based upon wishful thinking, but upon His sure promises. Thus, Heaven is promised to all who receive Him as Savior through faith in His name.

What a real comfort Heaven is when we know that, by contrast, death is an ever present reality. When my wife's grandmother died, the first thing Terry said to me about it was that it was wonderful to know that Grandma was in Heaven. There she is seeing Grandpa. She is visiting with her son, Terry's Dad, and with daughter Helen. Furthermore, Grandma's suffering is over. She is now comforted. She is at rest. She is at home with the saints and the Savior for eternity.

Now, to me, it is more important to consider the reality of Heaven than whether Jesus can hit a golf ball 300 miles and "steer" it to the hole on the green.

However, logic suggests strongly to me that I be prayerfully quick to volunteer to be Jesus' partner if He ever decided to play in a golf scramble. Great time of day! He might even help me by steering some of my shots! Hmm…I wonder if Tiger Woods…..?

"DOES GOD NUMBER THE HAIRS IN OUR NOSE?"

One night while I was reading, Jamin, seven-years old at the time, entered our bedroom and plopped across the bed.

I looked at him, and he grinned sheepishly.

"What's on your mind, son?" I asked.

He rolled over onto his back, and replied, "Nothing."

I went back to reading, and he lay looking at the ceiling for several minutes.

Finally, he broke the silence, "Dad, I have a question? Does God number the hairs in our nose?"

His question literally cracked me up, making me laugh long and loud. I know what the Scripture says about God numbering the hairs on our head, but it has never, ever occurred to me to consider the question from the perspective of the probosis.

After all, most of us are more concerned about the cranial count than the narial count. Furthermore, head hair far exceeds nose hair on everyone's standards for attractiveness. Who ever gets complimented on having a brushy beak?

Despite its humorousness, Jamin's concern only underscores the multitude of questions that people have concerning God.

Children's questions concerning God are often thought provoking. By contrast, questions from adults concerning God are most often filled with bitterness, doubt, and accusation. Some are even spewed arrogantly against God.

But, has it occurred to you that God, too, has some biting questions with which He confronts us?

For instance, consider the question, which God certainly directs to people of every generation, "What think ye of Christ?"

If we are going to bombard God with questions, we better realize that, some how, some way, and at some time, He is going to counter our questions with one of His own about our perspective of the person of Jesus Christ.

His Son was no ordinary man. He was more than just a gifted teacher. Every passage of Scripture pointing to Jesus Christ illuminates His divinity. Every work and word of Jesus Christ recorded in the Bible describes Him to be the ultimate revelation of God manifested in the flesh. "In the beginning was the Word, and the Word with God, and the Word was God."

Jesus Christ could be no less if He were to supremely provide the sacrifice alone necessary for our sins, which leads us to another biting question God directs to us.

"How shall we escape, if we neglect so great salvation?"

In general, there are two things that astound me about the mind-sets of people. First, as it deals mostly with the young, many have the attitude that they will live forever. Second, many who know they will not live forever still seem ambivalent about eternity.

As it concerns the former, it is sure that our individual lives will come to an end at some point. We cannot escape it. It is appointed unto man once to die.

But, since that is the case, why should we neglect, put off, or deny the wonderful salvation God has provided through the redemptive work of His Son, Jesus Christ?

We cannot escape the ramifications of eternal death if we neglect salvation. We have no eternal hope for Heaven when we die if we neglect salvation. We cannot avoid judgment if we neglect salvation.

No wonder God fires questions back at us. He does so with loving purpose. He is not just trying to be nosy about it, either.

We may ask God a thousand questions. But, His to us are the most consequential.

10

GOD HELPS US TO GRIEVE WELL

○ ○

"BY THE SADNESS OF THE COUNTENANCE THE HEART IS MADE BETTER"

—(ECCLESIASTES 7:3)

GOD WAS STILL GREAT IN THE SECOND WRECK!

I have heard it sometimes said by different people, "Parents should not have to bury their children."

Terry and I never thought we would have to bury one our boys, but the time certainly came in which we had to bury our third son, Eran. He was nineteen years old. He died August 9th, 2002. We buried his body three days later on August 12th.

The funeral home director said that, in his estimation, it was the second largest funeral he had ever worked. Four hundred and fifty people crowded our church sanctuary for the funeral. Over a thousand paid respects at the funeral home.

Eran was a great kid. He was handsome in his appearance. He was intelligent and athletic. He was kind, but sometimes moody and easily temperamental. As he became an older teenager, it was pleasing to notice how much he enjoyed working with children. He garnered respect from those who knew him. Eran had set his vocational goal to study and become a psychiatrist. He had achieved excellently throughout high school, and expectations for success and happiness in life were high.

We observed about him, however, that it seemed as though he was prone to accidents. Once, he fell twelve feet onto his back. He got mauled by two dogs. He thoughtlessly opened the door to our slowing vehicle, and fell out. He was struck in the head by a golf club carelessly swung by his brother. He wrecked an employer's delivery vehicle. He totaled two cars.

Nonetheless, it was purposeful that this compilation began with "The Wreck." We rejoiced how God had seen fit to spare Eran and his companion, Kate Lowe, from that horrific accident. We praised God for His greatness in the aftermath of the first wreck.

But, then there was that second wreck. God did not see fit to spare Eran's life in that second wreck. Would it not stand to reason that God's greatness became seriously diminished in our perspective because of it?

The question at hand, therefore, as it involves the will and work of God, is what conditions must be met in our personal estimations for God to be great. Is the greatness of God to be limited to only those circumstances when life and property are delivered from death and destruction? Or, is God great, too, though times are when He allows bad things to happen to His people?

Here is what I discovered about the greatness of God as it concerned that second wreck in which our third-born son died.

First, God is always great, and it was my duty to regard God as great. I am a believer in Jesus Christ, through whom He was great at Calvary. He was great in the Resurrection, through which He conquered death, hell, and the grave, making an eternal difference. Because I am a child of God, it is my duty to consider God great at all times and in all circumstances.

Second, God is always great, and it was my desire to regard God as great. We needed God. We desperately needed His great consolation, great assurance, and great peace. He has been absolutely great in responding to our desire for Him to be great with those great graces.

God was particularly great in the funeral service at Faith Baptist Church. As I sang with the congregation the hymn "How Great Thou Art," I found myself focusing on worship of God so much that I momentarily forgot that my son's body was in the closed casket before me. Words cannot adequately describe how contact with God through worship strengthened my soul.

Third, God is always great, and it is my delight to regard God as great. He taught me to grieve well as under-girded by absolute trust in God. He has allowed me to cry, but has reminded me to not dwell on Eran. Times when my sleep is disturbed concerning Eran, God restores my sleep. When I think about Eran being dead, God reminds me that my boy is alive with Him.

I have sincerely seized the opportunity to experience more of God through the death of our son. If you are willing to always trust God, you will always find Him to be great when human tragedy befalls us.

WE ARE EXPERIENCING A WONDERFUL GRIEF

August 9th, 2002 marked the 27th year that Terry and I have been married. And, it also marked the first day that our son, Eran, spent in Heaven with the Lord.

Eran, the third born of our six sons, was killed in a car accident early that Friday morning. It was 7:07 AM when we received notice of his accident. We buried his body on the following Monday.

With the passion of my soul, I assure you that my family and I are experiencing a wonderful grief. The strength and power of God are very real for those who trust Him supremely, as we most certainly do.

We are experiencing a wonderful grief because we know we have not lost Eran—we know where He is.

Undoubtedly, the reference to the "loss of a loved one" is embedded in our perspective about death. But, God has promised Christians eternal life in Heaven with Him. I had the privilege of leading Eran to receive Christ as his Savior. The Scripture assures us that to be absent from the body is to be present with the Lord. Eran certainly is not with us, but we know that he is with God, and that helps make our grief wonderful.

We are experiencing a wonderful grief because of the assurance we have from God that Eran lived a full life. Oh, yes, he was only 19 years old. But, he lived a full life because he lived the extent of life God wanted him to live. All of the life God wanted our family to have with him we had. Eran scored every touchdown on the field, made every A in the classroom, and achieved every goal before him that God intended.

We exchanged with him every "I love you," every word of encouragement, and every moment of strong family relationship. Because of that understanding, we approached his casket with no regrets. We can say that, with Eran, we had the fullness of family.

We are experiencing a wonderful grief because Eran did not die alone. The thought that I was not present with my son as he experienced death was a thought that came close to breaking me. But, God reminded me that Eran was not alone. God was with my boy to make that eternal transition. God stood by my boy, lifting him from his broken physical body to clothe him with one fit for Heaven. God is faithful to me because He was faithful to my son in his dying moment. I find great consolation because of it.

I told many people over the days following that my pain is from the neck upward. There has been pain in my jaw and in my eyes in the times I have cried from the grief. There is pain even now as I think about the reality of what has happened.

But, there is no pain in my heart. The reason it is true is because God is still being wonderful. His strength is a wonderful sedative to my soul. His peace is a present help in this time of need. His grace is amazing.

You see, this wonderful grief is possible because of the death and resurrection of Jesus Christ, because of the real and abiding presence of the Holy Spirit, because of the authoritative and absolute power of Almighty God, and because of the soothing comfort of His Word.

"Blessed be God, even the Father of our Lord Jesus Christ, the Father of mercies, and the God of all comfort, who comforteth us in all our tribulation."

August 9th will always be a day of celebration for Terry and me. It will not only be a remembrance of our wonderful marriage, but also a wonderful remembrance of the day our Eran went to Heaven.

DOES HE KNOW YOU LOVE HIM?

After we all had had a good cry around Eran's casket August 11th at the Foglesong-Tucker funeral home in Mason, Keithen told us a story that gave us a good laugh.

Eran was very affectionate. He often loved on his mother, telling her he loved her. He hugged on the rest of us guys, too. It was good, but Keithen was sometimes reserved about it.

There was a time when Eran got Keithen in a wrestling hold, and said, "I'm not going to let you go until you say you love me, too." Keithen did not budge, and Eran eventually wore out first!

One night when these two were going to be by themselves at the house, Eran pulled a prank on Keithen, which, as it turned out, evoked a powerful response proving emphatically his brotherly love.

Eran took one of those capsules with fake blood, and cracked it in his mouth. He also took ketchup and smeared it all over the front of his tee shirt. About the time that Keithen pulled into the driveway, Eran placed a ketchup-stained knife on the floor, and lay down beside of it.

As Keithen stepped through the door, he was utterly shocked at the sight. He ran and fell down beside of Eran.

"Eran! Eran!" Keithen yelled as he vigorously shook Eran.

Eran held on for as long as he could. He finally opened his eyes, and started laughing uncontrollably. Keithen reeled backward in confusion.

After Eran got control of himself, he thrust his finger into Keithen's face and said, "I knew you loved me!"

After having heard the story, I think Eran may have planned his prank to skirt the edge too closely. But, in retrospect, it does rip open a question on two accounts to put our personal accountability into serious perspective.

First, what will it take before your spouse, your children, or your parents know from you that you love them?

Regrettably, it all too often takes some sort of tragic event before we attempt to communicate our love for family to family.

The sweetest experience of life is the privilege to live daily knowing that you are under the banner of a family member's love. It prevails upon us personally, therefore, to always impress this assurance on our family members by way of attitude or action, because we never know when it will be too late to let them know. Otherwise, there is bitter regret with which to deal.

But, the greater question to confront us is, "Does Christ know that you love Him?"

Immediately, our Scriptural attention is drawn to when the Lord asked Peter, "Do you love me?" Jesus posed the question three times to His disciple during that dynamic interchange.

But, how is it that we communicate to the Lord that we love Him? This broad consideration may be narrowed to one statement by Him, "If a man love me, He will keep my words" (John 14:23).

After all, He has proven to us that He loves us. He did not lie down on a floor, but on a Cross to prove His love. He did not use the prop of a detached knife, but was propped on the Cross by three spikes attached to Him. He did not fake a bloody body, but rather the blood He shed was real—it was His personal blood that was shed for our eternal redemption.

He wants to know if you love Him for what He did for you? Do you not think that is a reasonable expectation?

For sure, Keithen showed Eran he loved him. We all loved Eran. We are thankful that he dwells in Heavenly safety.

"I TALKED TO ERAN LAST NIGHT"
(10-28-02)

I have certainly thought about the issue of human grief since August 9th when our third son, Eran, was killed in a car accident. It has been twelve weeks now to this point.

Grief is, undoubtedly, a gift from God to help us release that inward pain of the soul and spirit. "For by the sadness of the countenance the heart is made better," states the Scripture. It is most appropriate to grieve when it is required of us.

But, grieving well is the rub. For Christians, an important facet of grieving well must be the holding onto the truths of God's Word. Grief under-girded with the preciousness of sure hope stabilizes the soul.

I could not sleep the night of Eran's birthday, September 15th, because he consumed my thoughts. During that early morning hour, God's amazing grace once again brought comfort as I wrote the following:

I TALKED TO ERAN LAST NIGHT
(September 15, 2002)

I talked to Eran last night.
I don't know why I admit it, because I know he really wasn't there.
Besides, I didn't verbalize anything. I just visualized about talking to him.
But, I sure wish I could talk to him right now.
I miss having my boy here.
It was such a good life with him here.
Oh, he was testy for a couple of years,
but it was just standard procedure for a growing young man.
I lost my temper very badly with him one
time when he tried to stand up to me on a
disciplinary concern. Though I am not
proud of how badly I responded, I don't
regret it. According to his own admission,
the incident made him realize how necessary
it was for him to make some personal
adjustments for himself and the sake of his family.
He was good at making adjustments.
He was adamant about not wanting to
move from St. Marys to Mason in 1998. It
took him a while to accept it. He certainly
growled about it. But, when he made up his
mind that God was in it, he embraced it and made the best of it.
He did not want to make the change on
offense from fullback to quarterback for the
Falcon's football team. But, his team needed
him to play the position, and he made the
adjustment. He did it to the best of his
ability, sacrificing personal goals for the sake of the team.
Now—with that car accident of his—he has
made the ultimate adjustment.
And, it leaves me with having to face
adjustment, too. It is the hardest adjustment

I have ever had to make.
But, bless his soul, he made the adjustment
when discipline expected it.
He made the adjustment when I asked him to move.
He made the adjustment when his team asked him to play quarterback.
He made the adjustment to Heaven because our God required it of him.
Thank God how He is helping me to adjust,
and, as I think about Eran's capability to adjust,
I find a new measure of comfort for my soul.
And, really, it is not so hard to make the
adjustment just so long I keep in mind that it is
merely making adjustment to his new living situation.
No. I really didn't talk to Eran. He was just
on my mind so much tonight.

"Pap"

Grieving well for the Christian means refraining from being overly sentimental and from being overly concerned with what could have been.

But, more importantly, grieving well means trusting the assurances of our Lord Jesus Christ.

"You believe in God, believe also in me," He said.

After I finished writing, I went back to bed, and God gave me sleep.

REMEMBER THE SON

A month before Christmas 2002, I told my family that I wanted each of us to write down little memories of Eran, the third of the Branch sons who was nineteen years old when he went to Heaven August 9th, 2002.

There is no question that we will not ever forget him, but those seemingly insignificant, yet precious, memories of him may find occasion to fade from us with the passing of time. We do not want to lose mental and emotional touch with those routine remembrances that will, in years to come, stimulate smiles and feelings of warmth concerning him. As a matter of fact, certain matters concerning Eran were starting to escape from my own mind before we began this little family exercise.

For example, Keithen wrote, "In baseball at St. Marys High School, Eran and I held down the outfield. Usually coach asked me before the game what outfield position I wanted to play that day. I always took the best position with respect to the sun. Eran asked me one day why coach always placed him with the sun in his eyes. I just shrugged it off and acted like I didn't know!"

These types of memories serve for the present, and will for the future, as measures of comfort to our family.

Nonetheless, there we were as a family, our souls still sore from a harsh, unforgettable fact, stepping through the days of that initial Christmas celebration, and faced with such a displeasing reality when, in the past, there had been so much joy in our wholeness.

In no uncertain terms, grief etches on our faith like the scratching marks of sand on glass.

Yet, it is clear there is a higher plane of experience and perspective which should prevail on, not only the Branch family, but all other families whose cherished loved ones will never again be present to celebrate Christmas.

And, it goes right back to the to this concept to remember the son.

The predominant encouragement from God's Word directs us to, "Remember Jesus Christ of the seed of David."

There it is! Remember the Son. Above all else, remember the Son. Despite the grind of grief, remember the Son, for in remembrance of Him there is always present hope and peace for troubled and throbbing hearts and minds.

Words are not capable of describing how valuable it is to me that, as I remember the son, I remember the Son.

This is where the Scripture is so important, because in one respect, it is God's particular notes of remembrance about His own Son when the Son had been taken away by necessity. Indeed, that first Christmas for God without His Son by His side was most surely an unsavory experience. But, He wrote down the necessary points of remembrance, which should not be forgotten with the passage of time.

He wrote down the rigors of His Son's incarnate experience. The birth into poor circumstances was demeaning. He was born in a barn, and placed in a feed trough. The persistent threat of death swirled about His birth.

God also wrote down the joys by which to remember the Son. A special star guided three passionate men to His Son. Angels, in dramatic fashion, startled a group of shepherds with news about the Son's birth.

But, the undeniable purpose concerning the Son's departure is evident in God's Scriptural memoirs, "Blessed be the Lord God of Israel, for He hath visited and redeemed His people, and hath raised up an horn of salvation for us." Therein lies the prevailing comfort for us all.

Anyway, returning to our written remembrances, Jamin wrote how Eran and he would pull up their shirts, make stomach contact, and say, "Rub fat bellies!" That will be Jamin's special memory, because neither of us is going rub bellies with Jamin! Where do kids come up with stuff like that? My boys are something sometimes!

IT IS GOOD TO HAVE HIM REMEMBERED

"Hey, Ron!"

A gentle voice called to me from down in the hallway. The person was evidently not familiar where my study is located in our church.

"Down here," I replied as I rose from my desk to go to the door.

Once in the hallway, I recognized the visitor to be Pam Thompson, the lady I refer to as the world famous librarian. She had in her hands a potted flower, which she handed to me as she entered the study.

"Every Easter in our church, we place flowers in memory of family and friends. This flower is from our son, Steve, who placed it in memory of your son, Eran. Steve wanted Terry and you to have it."

The flower was a Grape Hyacinth. The blooms were blue-bodied, white-tipped, and bell-shaped, dangling from draping stems. Long, light-green leaves intensified the impact of the hyacinth's presence. The pot was wrapped in bright, gold-colored paper.

One thing I have noted about grief is how comforting it is to have Eran remembered. There is something in my soul that does not want my boy to be forgotten, not from the standpoint of perpetual pity, but because of the extreme value of his life to my family and me.

That is why I am so grateful to Steve Thompson for choosing to remember Eran at Easter 2003 in his church. It became my special blessing from the Lord for that particular day.

But, if there is meaning to having my son remembered, why should not the same be true for God concerning His Son, Jesus Christ?

Says the Scripture, "Remember that Jesus Christ of the seed of David was raised from the dead." We are called to remember that Christ died on the Cross for us, and that He was raised from the dead to plow out of the way any spiritual hindrance to salvation and fellowship with God. "If I live, you shall live also," Jesus said. It is, therefore, good to have Him remembered.

But, there is something that garners emphasis concerning it. "Remember" refers to "an unassisted recalling," which really gets the wind flying in our face.

What is being suggested strongly to us is that we should not need any prompting to remember the Lord. God is not concerned about our remembering His Son from the standpoint of temporal pity and mental acquiescence often displayed only on special occasions, like the Easter season, for example.

Rather, it is good to have Him remembered because of the extreme value of His sacrificed and risen life.

The question occurs to me if God is not often righteously indignant with those who find it so inconvenient to remember His Son. Should we not reciprocate the love of God for us by remembering His Son?

It prevails upon us to remember that remembering requires active participation. If worship, commitment, and faithfulness are drags to your life, then you have a serious spiritual shortage, which needs to be addressed post-haste.

The last time I saw Eran alive was as I walked with him out to the car. As he started down the driveway, he called out, "Bye, Pap! I'll see you tomorrow!"

When Eran died, he got to a tomorrow that I have not gotten to just yet. But, I remember his words with the same anticipation today as I had then.

I will most definitely see my boy tomorrow, but it is good to remember most the One who makes that tomorrow so definite.

More than ever before do I rejoice in remembering the Lord Jesus Christ. It is just impossible to describe how meaningful it is today until I get to that tomorrow!

Steve Thompson—you did a good thing for the Branch family.

GOOD GRIEF IS A GOD SEND
(8-9-03)

Recently, our oldest son, Ron, composed words and music to a song in memory of brother, Eran, who died August 9th, 2002.

Verse one goes, "Your life here on earth is through, God has called you home. Even though I'm glad for you, my pain lingers on. I miss your face and the joy you would bring. I miss hearing you laugh, and hearing you sing."

The second verse is, "You know I still think of you and I miss you every day. Sometimes it doesn't seem quite fair that it ended up this way. But I know God has His plan, and He's in control. And, I'll see you again someday, I know."

The chorus, "But I can't ask you to give up Heaven now. And I know that you would not come back even if you could some how. I can see you walking on Heaven's shores, and down streets of solid gold. Still I am left to miss you here until my dying day, I know. So, when God decides to call me home, two things I just want to do—first, I want to meet my Savior, then sing His praise with you."

Good grief is a God send since Eran died. Ron's song, in its combination of humanity and faith, speaks for us that we have been experiencing good grief during this past year.

Grief is a remarkable gift God has given to help us deal with the reality of life and death. When a significant loved one dies, good grief allows us to release that horrid inner pain. As Scripture suggests, "Sorrow is better than laughter, for the by the sadness of the countenance the heart is made better."

Unfortunately, some people go to the extreme of doing everything to avoid grief, while others dwell too much on grief. Such grief will rot your soul if you allow it. But, God does not want that to happen to us.

Therefore, what is good grief? How shall we grieve well? Here is what has been helpful to me.

Absolutely trust God. Quite honestly, if it were not for being able to trust God, I would not have anything to do with God. But, God continually proves that He can be trusted, especially as it concerns the promise and provision of Heaven. It is the Heavenly hope He gives that effectively assuages simmering anger and searing disappointment. Because of Heaven's assurance, we can know that our loved ones who are in Christ live in a blessed living environment. It is imperative to adjust to the fact of their new living arrangement provided by God. There is great consolation found in it to aid the process of grief.

Resolve to practice what you believe. A person thrust into grief and not willing to practice what they believe will have a more difficult experience. Practicing what we believe when it is particularly required provides a necessary source of solace for the soul. Too many grieving people abandon the moorings of what they previously professed to believe. Grief is only intensified when our spiritual beliefs are deliberately ignored or rejected.

Helpful to remember is that God's people do not die alone. The thought that Eran had to face death alone nearly broke me. But, in the moment my heart was crumbling, God reminded me He was with my boy for that time of eternal transition. God lifted my boy from his broken physical body to clothe him with one fit for Heaven. God was faithful to me because He was faithful to my son in his dying moment. I continue to find great consolation because of it.

Good grief embraces the spiritual truth that death is not a "loss." To my knowledge, there is nothing in Scripture that refers to the death of a saint as a "loss." Knowing our loved ones are alive with God in Heaven is as a balm being massaged into the spirit and soul.

One night just prior to the first anniversary of his death, I had a dream—so real in its visions—that God decided to bless us by letting us have Eran present with us during daylight hours. I was elated with the manifestation of his presence. I hugged on Eran, and talked with him so much. Our family was restored on earth in a most miraculous manner.

However, it abruptly ended when I asked, "Eran, what is eternity like?" It was as though God did not want that question answered. Then, I awoke from my wonderful dream, sensing a great abiding comfort that Eran was still with us, though aware his days were being lived in a better location.

I prayed, "Thank you, God. That was good." Then, I rolled over, and went back to sleep.

<u>"TO MOM...FROM ERAN"</u>

Men be warned! Do not ever throw away a woman's collection of gift bags. I threw away Terry's collection once, and, when she discovered what I had done, she lit into me with a quick lecture how those dainty, rattan-handled bags come in handy. To a woman, those things are revered.

When I came home the Tuesday afternoon before Christmas 2004, Terry was busy at the kitchen table wrapping Christmas purchases with her collection of gift bags she had saved over the last several—sigh—years.

Retrieving another gift bag from her huge gift poke, she stopped momentarily, then said, "Isn't this something? See the tag on this?"

Attached to the handle by a string was a tag on which was written, "To Mom...From Eran." This bag contained probably the last gift Eran had given his mother at Christmas three years ago.

The two of us spontaneously began to glow in the memories of our third son, who died two years and four months ago. Memories of him make us feel good.

Terry commented, "The thing that helps me most is that I believe his death was just a matter of God receiving him at the right time."

"My comfort is that he is still living—just in a different place, which is where God is," I replied.

Terry eventually folded up the bag, and set it off to the side. "Don't you dare throw this bag away!" she demanded sternly.

I clearly heard what she said. The gift bag had become special to us in that moment, because it had once served as wrapping for a gift that contributed to the joy of the Christmas season three years past. Upon discovery and realization, the significance of the gift bag did not break our hearts, but rather warmed our hearts as it prompted us with specific remembrances that keep us in touch with the reality of life we had with Eran. Consequently, it had become a fresh blessing in a unique way.

However, consider the purposeful contrast for us this very day as it involves the significance of Christmas. After all, God gave to mankind an inestimable gift in the person of His Son, Jesus Christ, 2000 years ago.

The purpose of God's gift has essentially been fulfilled. Christ was born and finished the work of redemption by way of the Cross and Resurrection. He presently sits at God's right hand providing intercession for us. Such lofty spiritual truths almost make it seem so far above us and unattainable in the perspectives of many.

But, what keeps us joyfully bound to the season is directly related to what is rediscovered in Scripture each year concerning the birth of Christ—"He was wrapped in swaddling clothes."

That is how God packaged the gift of His Son. God knew exactly what He was doing when He wrapped His Son the way He did. Christ was not wrapped in royalty but in swaddling clothes to give explicit explanation that the advantages of life in Christ is not just for a select few but for all.

And, it is from that point that we are stirred to cheering remembrances about God's Son, which keep us in touch with the reality of life we have in God through faith in Christ.

For example, the packaging of wrapping in swaddling clothes reminds us that the assurance of hope He gives is for all. The joy He gives is for all. The peace He gives is for all. The salvation He gives is for all.

In so many terms, the swaddling clothes serve as the tag, which says, "To You…From God."

By the way, I had a terrible nightmare last night. I dreamt that all I got for Christmas were bags of gift bags! It sure was good to finally wake up.

HEAVEN IS A PLACE WHERE WE WILL NEVER GROW OLD!

Two years later I still am a recovering griever.

Dealing well with grief often entails sifting through some emotional and spiritual sticking points. The Lord helped me through one of mine recently.

Since our third son, Eran, died, August 9th, 2002, I have not possessed the emotional stamina to gaze on our pictures of him. Shortly after the funeral, two great girls, Kate Lowe and Natalie Faulk, delivered to us a photo album they had lovingly compiled of Eran's athletic and social experiences at Wahama High School. It was such a thoughtful gesture directed toward our family, and we regard it as a valuable keepsake for us.

However, I have not yet been able to view it. I am spiritually comforted in most all aspects of the grief process. I continue to absolutely trust God. Yet, pictures of my boy strike down my soul.

The problem as it confronts me is that I will never see Eran older than nineteen years old. For whatever reason, that thought has been a sticking point for me in dealing with the experience of his death. Eventually, Eran's three younger brothers will surpass nineteen years of age. The rest of us will progress through the appearances of age, much of which will be captured on video and preserved by snapshots. But, it just does not seem right from my perspective to have to leave our third-born behind looking only nineteen. It has grieved me. I know it sounds trivial.

Nonetheless, I recently made a prayerful complaint to the Lord about it.

He startled me with His clear response, "Well, what's wrong with that?"

In that moment, the first verse of that great, old hymn came to mind, "I have heard of a land on the faraway strand, 'Tis a beautiful home of the soul. Built by Jesus on high, there we never shall die, 'Tis a land where we never grow old."

While I have no problem as such that Eran is where he will never grow old, why should I hang on to some point of useless grief that Eran will never look any older? Why should that not be acceptable to me as a good thing?

All of this continues to underscore for me the inestimable value of the hope of Heaven provided by Jesus Christ. Clearly, when one takes the harsh realities of life, and emotionally and spiritually allow them to be framed within the context of Heaven's hope, positive perspectives seem to seep into the soul to soothe the sore.

After all, Heaven, Scripturally described, is a place of thriving life. Heaven's inhabitants are no longer subjected to the ravages of disease, since it is a place where there is no more dying. No wonder they no longer advance in age.

Every quality of Heaven is designed by God to stimulate life. The river described there is one of life. The fountains described there are those of life. The tree of life is there. Above all, the One who is the source of life is there. Heaven is blessed with exuding life, and is completely devoid of the curse on the life we live here. No wonder Eran is no longer advancing in age. If he is still nineteen in Heaven, I have no reason to grieve that he will appear no older here.

You and I have experienced the same. God has seen fit that certain of our loved ones stop living with us to go live with Him. But, when we hold onto the sure hope of Heaven, it makes a vital contribution to dealing with grief in a way that glorifies Him who has provided such a wonderful hope to us.

I think I can take a good look at that picture album now.

11

GOD WANTS US TO BE VICTORIOUS

○ ○

"FOR WHATSOEVER IS BORN OF GOD OVERCOMETH THE WORLD: AND THIS IS THE VICTORY THAT OVERCOMETH THE WORLD, EVEN OUR FAITH"

—(I JOHN 5:4)

OVERCOME AND PREVAIL!

Revelation 2 and 3 contain the messages of Jesus Christ to the seven churches located in the cities of Ephesus, Smyrna, Pergamos, Thyatira, Sardis, Philadelphia, and Leodicea.

To each of these churches, our Lord gave specific promises "to him that overcometh." These promises involve immense spiritual value.

One who overcomes is one who prevails. Such is typical of the true believer in Jesus Christ, for a true believer is one who is faithful to the Lord from beginning to end in their profession of faith as a Christian.

As God's people, we continually stand in need of encouragement to stay steady and faithful. God knows that we continually need to be cheered onward.

In the Gospels, Jesus Christ said three times, "Be of good cheer!" Why? Because He knows human nature. He knows how we are prone to discouragement. We experience the blues. We feel defeated. Worthless at times. Downcast. Frustrated! Incompetent!! Unheard!!

Clearly, God cheers us on to be prevailers that overcome for victory.

When Keithen was twelve years old, he wrestled with a youth wrestling team known as the Cougars. I paid the price for him to be on the team. I provided the means for him to be on the team.

It was during the "Cougar Classic Tournament" that Keithen met in the finals his arch-opponent, a very good and well-known wrestler on the youth circuit that had dominated Keithen in other tournaments.

But, on this day, Keithen was really focused. I could tell. All day he had wrestled with an aggressive energy that I had not seen from him.

When our boys wrestle, I try to remain laid back and cool. I do not want to act foolishly like other adults do when their kids wrestle. But, this match was different for me as I felt with and for Keithen's effort perhaps more than ever.

At the end of the first period, the score was 4-4. Feeling the intensity building in me because of the display of fine competition, I was compelled to move from the stands to near the edge of the center-stage mat. I could not help it! Kneeling, I gestured encouragingly to him when he looked my direction.

For the start of the second period, Keithen won the toss, and elected to assume the up-position. At the sound of the ref's whistle, I called loud, enthusiastic encouragement for Keithen to do his best. Though he wrestled hard, his opponent scored a reversal. The second period ended with Keithen behind 6-4.

(At times, we feel ourselves behind in the scores of life, do we not?)

The third period began with Keithen in the down-position. When the whistle sounded, Keithen hit his moves hard. He looked determined.

After fifteen seconds, Keithen hit a reversal, gaining two points. It was 6-6.

Suddenly, he rolled his opponent onto his back into a pinning position.

I let the cheering rip from my heart and roar through my mouth, "HOLD ON, KEITHEN! PULL, KEITHEN! COME ON, KEITHEN!"

Keithen held onto his near-fall position. When time expired, the ref awarded Keithen the resulting three points. He won 9-6. He overcame. He prevailed.

The ref raised Keithen's hand to signify him as the winner. I was very proud, more so that he had been so determined to prevail. That is what counts.

Keithen walked toward me with that ear-to-ear grin of his. I threw out my arms. He threw out his arms. We embraced. And, leaving the gym, I found a secluded place and wept.

But, consider the powerful spiritual comparison. We have a Savior who paid the price for us to enter salvation's race. We have a Savior who provided us the means and the privilege to be on His team. Because of it, He expects us to give our best in the fight and the struggle.

All the while, however, He exhorts us to prevail. He encourages us to go on.

"Pull!" He calls.

"Hold on!" He calls.

"Come on! You can do it! I am with you!" He calls.

But, wait—you can hear clearly in the background that great cloud of witnesses, those who have gone on before us (Hebrews 12:1), who stand to exhort us onward, too.

"With His help, we overcame!" they call.

"With His help you, too, will overcome!" they call.

No cheer-leading squad in all the world can effectively cheer us on as these.

Saint, keep up the fight! Overcome and prevail!

And, by God's grace, you shall.

978-0-595-39356-5
0-595-39356-X